D0723712

The
Bhagavad
Gita
Revealed

The Bhagavad Gita Revealed

A Living Teaching for Our Times

Based on video presentations by Sat Shree
using portions of the Bhagavad Gita as translated
by Swami Sri Atmananda

by Sat Shree
Part 1: Journey to the Self

NEW DHARMA PUBLICATIONS

Copyrighted Material

The Bhagavad Gita Revealed: A Living Teaching for Our Times

Copyright © 2018 by New Dharma.
All Rights Reserved.

No part of this publication may be reproduced, stored in a retrieval system or trans-mitted, in any form or by any means—electronic, mechanical, photocopying, recording or otherwise—without prior written permission from New Dharma, except for the inclusion of brief quotations in a review.

For information about this title or to order other books and/or electronic media, contact the publisher:

New Dharma, a nonprofit organization
18124 Wedge Pkwy Suite 212
Reno, NV 89511
www.satshree.org
newdharma@gmail.com

Library of Congress Control Number in process

ISBNs:
Print: 978-1-7323059-0-8
eBook: 978-1-7323059-1-5

Printed in the United States of America

Cover design by Anita Soos, Anita Soos Design
Text and illustration design by Patty Arnold, Menagerie Design and Publishing

Publisher's Cataloging-In-Publication Data in process

I dedicate this revelation of the eternal teaching of the Bhagavad Gita to my spiritual father and guru, Swamiji Sri Atmananda. I knew nothing of the true spiritual journey, its purpose or outcome, before I met him. He not only guided and supported me but showed me that the Gita was a map, a step-by-step description of the spiritual journey. Through him I realized that the Gita is, in fact, a living spiritual reality that can activate a divine potentiality that lies latent in each of us. It is also evidence of a benign, intelligent Presence that holds and supports all of us throughout the twists and turns of our lives. The Bhagavad Gita is the Song of the Supreme, in the same way a mother sings to her child, bringing comfort, guidance and inspiration. It is a message of great hope for each of us, and for mankind.

Acknowledgements

This publication could not have come into existence without the loving sacrifice of a number of people for whom I feel a deep level of gratitude. They include Meera Weaver, husband Glenn Hovemann, Karen Kernan, and others who volunteered their time to read and give feedback on the manuscript. To all those whose loving sacrifice gave birth to this publication, I thank you for your support in this work.

Table of Contents

Awakening

My Story

Many spiritual awakenings are happening now. The elastic membrane of the collective consciousness has been pierced. It happened to me late one night in the early winter of 1998. From the beginning I knew that my awakening was not personal, was not random, and was not happening only to me. Although it took years to fully understand, from that moment on I experienced an extraordinary new consciousness that shifted my reality. It was a natural unfolding, a reflection of a shift in the collective consciousness. Many spiritual experiences and revelations followed.

Over time I was shown the purpose of life and the nature of the entire journey of consciousness. I saw that every awakening is purposeful and has a role to play in the unfolding of this new consciousness coming to the planet. I have since learned to articulate that which is actually known by all of us, but at levels beyond the reach of our normal consciousness. I am here to share the purpose of life and the path to its fulfillment as it has been revealed within me.

How It All Began

I was not a spiritual seeker before my awakening. I was an architect, community activist, and part-owner of a solar energy company. Married with two children, I lacked nothing.

But late one evening, on January 4th, as my brother was leaving after a visit, a great sadness came over me because I had been too busy to spend time with him. Unexpectedly an immense anguish and grief erupted. All the loveless, unconscious acts of selfishness and insensitivity I had lived as a self-serving human being flooded my consciousness with great intensity.

Unknowingly I entered a new state of consciousness. An image of a perhaps past life flashed before me. I saw myself as a young boy in Germany in the early 1930s. I was in an open field on my family's farm and had just launched a wooden model airplane I had built. I was filled with amazement and great joy. Then, in another flash, I saw myself ten years later as a Nazi soldier, intoxicated with power, hurling Jews onto a train bound for a concentration camp. The shame and horror at seeing this capacity for evil and cruelty toward others and my complete indifference to human suffering was so overwhelming that I literally went unconscious, collapsing forward onto my drafting board.

When I awoke, as I looked out over the high desert where I lived, the whole universe revealed itself. I was standing in the middle of it, watching the stars age. I had broken through into a new dimension of being. I was connected with everything. I had no clue what was happening; only much later did I realize what it meant. But I knew, to my very core, that I had won the lottery of all lotteries. I began seeing the swirling forms of intelligent entities that constantly work to sustain this world and to support each of us. I knew to the core of my being that all they wanted was for each of us to awaken as I was awakening. "Everything matters! We are all interconnected!"

Overwhelmed, humbled, and in awe, I saw that there is so much more to this existence and our human lives than we can ever know. It was very clear to me that this experience was not about my deserving it; it had not come because of anything I had done or was doing. Rather, something was happening spontaneously. Somehow I knew it to be the result of a natural process that is the birthright of all of us. It is a process we will each experience in the course of our many lives—whether we know it or not.

Over the next few months these experiences continued. I kept trying to make sense of what was happening. My wife and I did research and talked to friends, but it wasn't until I went to a small nearby ashram in northern Nevada that something clicked. I became aware of an Indian teacher, Sri Atmananda, whose main ashram was in southern India at the foot of a sacred mountain called Arunachala. I was given a videotape about him to watch. As soon as the tape began to play, a deep recognition seized me. I knew that what I was seeing in Sri Atmananda was the culmination of what had started in me. This threw me into a state of divine intoxication for the next thirty-six hours. It only quieted when I heard, through one of his students, his assurance that what was happening for me was real, that he knew of me, and that I was destined to attain *jivan mukti,* or liberation, while living. My entire system immediately calmed; I knew I had found my track. He was to become my guru. So began my nine-year process that culminated in the realization of God and Truth.

While I waited some nine months for Sri Atmananda to come to the United States, I purposefully and responsibly closed out my life as I had known it. After his short visit I returned with him to India, without looking back. I spent most of the six years from 1998 to 2004 with him in India. My awakening continued to unfold during this period. It was an endless process, revealing deeper and deeper dimensions of the spiritual domains as well as the dark recesses and resistances of individual ego and shared collective conditioning. My teacher introduced me to the rich spiritual traditions of India—especially the Bhagavad Gita, a living scripture that reveals the highest spiritual truths and has guided souls on the inner path for millennia. I found in the Gita a direct link to my experiences and a clear description of the many different stages of the journey on which I was traveling.

SAMADHI

In 2004 my teacher deemed me ready, gave me a spiritual name, and sent me back to the United States to open a small spiritual center. One day something unexpected began happening. I became totally absorbed in a condition of consciousness I had not previously known. It gripped all parts of my being. My awareness froze. All thought was gone. The world disappeared. My body became completely still—no movement, no digestion, no breath—for up to thirty-six hours at a time. Later I learned these were *nirvikalpa samadhi* states. I was merging with the Absolute. These states continued to come and go for three and a half years. Each time I emerged from this samadhi I struggled to gather myself together, as everything in me wanted to stay absorbed. But over time I became skillful at moving between these deep states and normal consciousness. I became capable of fulfilling my function in the world.

THE FINAL REALIZATION

One day in the summer of 2007 the final realization came. It was as plain as day. I realized that I was—as all of us are—what is called "God" or the "Absolute"—the eternal Reality. At that moment a fundamental shift occurred that has never gone away, but rather has grown over the years. For me at that moment all seeking was over. It was done, complete. There was no longer a student or a teacher. What I had made important or "real" in the course of my entire life, and even since my awakening, was shown to be merely temporary scaffolding that has to be stripped away in the end.

There is only *this*, an unspeakable *is-ness*. I knew my true nature as pure Presence, the context for the content of Life. I knew this without any doubt or ambiguity. That which I am is an impersonal instrument or channel for the Universe to express itself. This I saw plainly and clearly. I had traveled all of the stages of the soul's journey and had returned back to my original nature. I knew that all living beings share this ancient, archetypal journey.

With this realization came the awareness that all I had been doing as a spiritual teacher up until that moment had to end; I could not continue to do what I had been doing. Over the next year I carefully completed this aspect of my life, handing over the work of the spiritual center to others. I left and began living alone in a small room above a daycare center in Olympia, Washington. I was completely fulfilled. Nothing was missing. Nothing was needed.

Manifestation

After a time the next phase began. In 2009 I moved back to Washoe Valley, Nevada, and began work that was aligned with the new consciousness that had come. I took the name Sat Shree, and with my wife Satyamayi, who was also a devotee of Atmananda, formed a nonprofit corporation called New Dharma. Since that time I have developed a language to describe the spiritual journey that matches my experience as a Westerner. Over the years, I have developed methods that accelerate the spiritual process for those who are ready to progress.

I have become a crack in the Universe, a fracture in the Creation. I am a void into which things that are not true dissolve and disappear forever, and out of which the new and real and true is born. For me this is now normal. It is the clear, plain truth of what I am. Very few know how to be with "what" I have become. It is not their fault. They, too, are this at their core; but this reality is veiled because human beings are conditioned, programmed, trained to take on and create egoic content. We are driven to be a "who"—an individual person—a construct which does have a role to play in the journey of consciousness. As the journey continues, however, this role becomes a hindrance and must be released and dissolved. With that dissolution a new way of being—a new dharma—can begin to manifest. This work of individual transformation is especially needed in these times to support the shift in the collective consciousness that is under way.

THE INVITATION

My mission is to assist people in reaching their highest possibility so they can play their part in this shift. This is not something I do; rather it is an opportunity that arises spontaneously from "what" I am. I invite all to grow into the realization of this "whatness" and share this opportunity. I represent a new possibility of being that is available to all of humanity.

It is time to get out of your little mopey story about yourself. It is time to take a stand for truth and to bring something "real" into existence. To come out of the bullshit, out of the lie we've been living. To drop the subterfuge, deception, bigotry, hypocrisy, ignorance, hatred, distortions, and belief systems that have locked human consciousness for millennia into ignorance and suffering. We each carry a piece of this collective error. Through our ancestral karma, through our choices, we perpetuate this error. It is only when we become capable of taking responsibility for our piece of the collective error that we can be useful in playing our part to bring this shift of consciousness into the collective. The more awake you are, the greater your responsibility.

Why do this? Because of our love of mankind. Because of our love of this world. It is a huge love. There can be no greater undertaking than to give ourselves over to such work. To serve it in whatever way we can, with whatever capacity we have. To pray for the ability to expand our capacity, and make that our mission. We do this not for security, or comfort, or the assurance of a good death, not even for enlightenment. We do this to be useful, to serve the world.

This is the New Dharma I bring. It is also the original dharma. It is the absolute willingness to bring something totally new into existence. It is the resolve to bring this original condition of being into time and space, the here and now. I invite you to join me.

THE BHAGAVAD GITA

I use the Bhagavad Gita as a framework for my teaching. The Gita, the Celestial Song, is the essence of the perennial wisdom of the Universe. It is a dialogue between Arjuna, a noble warrior, and Krishna, his charioteer, who represents our inner Guru, our divine compass. It maps the final stages of this eternal journey of consciousness that each of us is traveling, whether aware of it or not. It describes a universal structure that exists not just in its story or in my revelation of it, but as a reflection of the eternal principles of truth and love—the absolute, unchanging, eternal reality—and the interconnected oneness of Creation.

The Gita is my path, although I didn't discover it until I was well along on the journey. The Gita showed me that I was on a journey, a journey with a beginning, a middle, and an end. It made clear to me that there are important stages and real transitions in this journey—like the "point of no return" where you can't come back to the world again in your old conditioned ways.

The Bhagavad Gita describes both a path of transcendence and a path of transformation. Both paths are to be lived. It illustrates and engenders within us a new state of being, a new way to live—what I call the New Dharma. The Gita taps into the primordial archetypal structure that is the foundation of all existence and reveals the purpose of human life. It is a living scripture that offers a new paradigm for being, and for living the new consciousness now coming to the planet. We share this journey, this path, this new way. We are all in this together. We are all interconnected. Each of us matters. Each of us has a part to play.

As you read the Gita, let it sink in at whatever level you can. The more you can simply absorb it, the more you become simple, the more you become humble, quiet, and still, the more it will nurture you. You, too, will become the remembrance. You, too, will become the Song, like the Gita itself. You will be a song of remembrance. Your very words will carry remembrance to those who can receive it. As I sing the Song of the Supreme to each of you, the Gita is reborn. The great wonder of the Gita is that it creates a new Gita with each of us, with every Arjuna and Arjuni.

Love in Truth,
Sat Shree

The basis for this book are Sat Shree's videos of the first six chapters of the Bhagavad Gita. These videos are accessible at no charge on his website, www.newdharma.org.

The Journey of Consciousness

We are all basically consciousness. Our original nature is pure, unadulterated truth—consciousness—presence. These are all words describing the same quality. But initially consciousness had no identity, no sense of itself. It was pure, wide-open consciousness. It only began to experience itself when it descended out of its original quiescent condition into domains of greater and greater density of matter. Then it became identified with matter, forgot its original nature, and identified with each material form it merged with. At the culmination of this evolutionary process, it became a human being who woke up in matter—matter waking up to itself. Consciousness believes it is its thoughts, its body, its feelings, its sensations, its story, and its beliefs. Over many lifetimes—birth, death, birth, death—eventually this identification with matter gradually weakens until it begins to disengage.

The Bhagavad Gita, the Song of the Supreme, begins at this point. It maps the spiritual journey wherein the human with self-awareness turns its attention inward to its source. It is a compelling story. It is truly a hero's journey of return to the source of what we really have been all along. The Gita describes the final stages of this dramatic story. It is our story; it is your story. But first we must set the stage for the Gita by creating an overall context, which I call the journey of consciousness.

We are all on a journey of consciousness, whether we know it or not. It begins with gaining information and insights into the nature and purpose of existence. We are all by-products of an evolutionary process that has a beginning, middle, and end. But there are fundamental factors, forces, structures, and mechanisms that cannot be seen behind the veil of ignorance that shrouds us all. Knowing the nature of the journey and where you are on it will allow you to be a collaborator in this miraculous unfolding of our innate reality that we call life.

All that we know, experience, and are is due to forces that have been at work since the beginning of time. We are all riding a Current of Becoming that is purposeful. It is the creative expression of the Original Intent inherent in the unmanifest potentiality which some call God or Truth.

A Map of the Journey

I have mapped the entire journey of consciousness. It is still a theory, but it is based on my direct experience. It is like a story, a useful story; what you might call a theory of everything. In my experience we are all the by-products of a purposeful evolutionary process. There are fundamental stages, aspects, forces, structures, and mechanisms that define this journey and lie behind the veil of our ordinary consciousness. These cannot be seen because of a veil of ignorance that shrouds us all. Having correct information about these things can thin this veil and allow us to be more effective collaborators in this miraculous revelation of the inherent possibility we all carry.

We strive to be happy but often just try to get by without too much suffering or pain. I call it lizard mentality. If you can get home without being eaten, it's been a good day. But when we live life aligned with the universe's purpose for us, we ride a current of becoming that is of a different order. It is a primal impulse that lies inherent in the Original Reality that is the source of all. It is the *will to be* that creates Life. When we tap in to this current we discover a new way to be in life, a new reality for being. This is the creative expression of what I call the Original Intent. This is the purpose of the Universe: *to be*, to exist, to experience, to know, to grow, to evolve, to learn, to develop, and ultimately to *wake up* to itself as each of us. This is the inherent drive of existence.

I have created a diagram that maps this journey with its stages and structures. (See Appendix I for a map detailing the journey.) There are four stages: the Descent into Creation, the Evolution, the Return Journey, and the Manifestation. In my cosmology there are primal structures and mechanisms of the one Original Reality that together are the cause of existence and that hold things in place. This one Reality has four separate modes of expression. This is a paradox. They are *Sat, Tat, Chit,* and *Ananda.* I am going to describe these structures in the simplest language that I can. These structures are the scaffolding by which the purpose can manifest itself into creation. You can find references for this in the Vedas and from world teachers like Meher Baba and Sri Aurobindo. There are similarities in their teachings to what I describe, but for me this whole cosmology appeared spontaneously. It appeared as a whole, as if it had always been there, although it has become more clear and concise as I have developed as a spiritual being and have been teaching. I invite you to use this map to understand the context for the predicament we are born into.

The Cause

"In the beginning . . ."

There are four aspects of the One Original Reality that together are the cause of existence and this journey of consciousness. They are Sat, Tat, Chit, and Ananda.

Sat is the Absolute. It is beyond all qualities. It cannot be described other than THAT which allows Existence. The nature of the Sat is that by itself it does nothing, ever; it is not a doer. It is the foundation. It is the nothing for the everything, the light on the screen that allows the movie. It is like an explosion of consciousness that is about ready to happen. It is a huge potentiality. It is the Self-Existing Existence. Not separate from the Sat is the *Asat,* like the light and dark side of the moon. They are, in fact, the same thing. In the timeless now the Asat and the Sat opened and became as two. In the breach between the two came a tension in which all of existence came into being. The Asat is the dark version of the Sat, the inherent potentiality of consciousness lost in matter, completely embedded in the densest, most inconscient, the most deeply unconscious condition of existence, and struggling to reemerge through evolution.

Tat is Creation. It holds the space for the manifestation of the infinite potentiality of the Sat. It is the domain of all Matter. It is Duality, Space and Time, Cause and Effect. It holds it all together, allowing what we know as manifest existence.

Chit is consciousness. It is the radiant manifestation of the Sat into the Tat. It is the Shakti, the animating force of Creation. When Chit becomes entangled with Tat, it manifests all the living forms and is the evolutionary force that eventually allows matter to wake up and become an individual self-aware soul or being.

Ananda is the enchantment of Existence. It is the Chit (consciousness) that experiences the Ananda. Ananda isn't just bliss. It is every moment when the consciousness encounters something other than itself. It loves to know and experience and make sense of it. It wants to figure out how to stay in Ananda forever.

These four principles are all expressions of the same One principle, and this is the cause of our existence.

The Stages of the Journey

Let's return to the diagram, The Journey of Consciousness, and follow the four stages. From the moment of its separation from the Sat, the Chit has been seeking a way back to its original state. But it has done so by looking outwardly for answers. It has no reference point, no basis for knowing where else to look. So it seeks to find its way in the outward domains of experience. This movement of seeking is the manifesting force of creation. This force wants to exist, to experience, and to know. Its purpose is *to be*; to learn, to evolve, and ultimately *to wake up* to its original nature.

The first stage of the journey is the Descent into Creation. The second stage is the Evolution, which develops more and more sophisticated vehicles for experience. The third stage is the Return Journey, where the Chit returns to its source. In this stage the Chit turns inward and begins to experience the Sat directly. The last stage is the Manifestation, wherein the awakened Chit consciously descends into Creation to assist in the manifestation of the Original Intent.

1. Descent

In this first phase consciousness expands, entangling itself with itself, creating what we call the planes of consciousness— the domains of existence that eventually materialize in the physical world. These domains range from subtle to gross. Those closer to the Sat are extremely subtle; those farther from the Sat take on density, shape, and form—the archetypes that in later stages form the physical creation as we know it.

2. Evolution

There are three stages of the evolutionary process: the formation of Matter, formation of Life, and formation of

Mind. Each builds on the other. Together they form the basis of the Creation.

Matter. In the first stage, raw consciousness entangles itself, creating more and more density and eventually precipitating into subatomic particles, then atoms, and then more and more complex atomic structures, leading to the phenomena of compounds such as chemicals and minerals. This leads to the creation of the physical universe. Consciousness is in its primal condition—raw energy descending into creation, forming the inconscient—an utterly unconscious condition.

Life. With Matter, consciousness now has the foundation for the next stage of evolution, the development of the living principle of existence. Consciousness now strives further, creating the early compounds of organic material. Creation bursts into innumerable forms and species, seeking to discover how to manifest the unlimited potentialities inherent in Sat. More and more forms capable of expressing the inherent consciousness more and more perfectly are created. Increasingly complex life forms emerge, forming an enormous range of elementary, plant, then animal life—each iteration becoming more complex and sophisticated, building on the lessons learned from previous experiments.

Mind. Mind developed as an inherent organizing principle imbedded in the Original Intent of the Sat to exist, to experience, to learn, and finally to wake up. This Mind principle developed concurrently with the development of Matter and Life. In the process, primitive mind came into existence. Viruses, bacteria, DNA, amino acids, cells, and more all "held" this organizing principle we are calling Mind, allowing for the lessons of the exuberant experimentation of creation to be recorded and stored for future use.

In this way, Life then evolved further, creating distinct independent forms and species, each with a primitive imperative to survive and succeed in fulfilling the unique opportunity it carried. Over time, Nature, as the expression of Chit, came closer and closer to creating an organism capable of manifesting consciousness. This process completed itself in the human being—an independent, self-aware vehicle for consciousness. With us, Nature has created a vehicle that can fulfill the Original Intent.

3. RETURN JOURNEY

When consciousness wakes up as a human being, a fundamental shift occurs in the journey of consciousness. Consciousness has fulfilled the Original Intent. It now has an enormous capacity to experience and to learn. It now exists as an awake self-aware individual with apparent free will and choice. All this arises due to the incredible sophistication and complexity of the human body. Chit—consciousness—has awakened as each one of us, but it is utterly identified with the human vehicle it occupies. It does not know its original nature. At this stage the outward seeking of the Chit is complete, but now it must dismantle its identification with the human form in which it woke up before it can begin the Return Journey.

The Return Journey has three interconnected stages. The first is the awakening of the inner Sat or soul within. Second is the undoing of our identification with the personality, body, and life in which we awoke. Third is the strengthening of the inner reality within until it overtakes the habit of our human nature. These three movements interact to reinforce each other, setting in motion a process that returns us to our original universal nature.

4. Manifestation

In rare cases when an individual soul has completed the journey and merged with the Sat, it returns to Creation to perform some function or mission. These souls are the great realized beings or avatars, such as Jesus, Buddha, Krishna, and Muhammad, who came to serve mankind. These beings accelerate the evolutionary process for the whole of creation, assisting in the manifestation of the Original Intent.

Many advanced souls may also reincarnate to do some specific work or fulfill some important function before they complete the journey. These lesser manifestations serve themselves and humanity at the same time, furthering their attainment while helping other souls complete the journey. These are the teachers, realized beings, saints, and gurus of the world.

The Gita's Map of Awakening

There are structures that exist in the subtle worlds, the worlds beyond our normal human boundaries, that are here for the purpose of supporting humanity in the evolution of consciousness. These are archetypal structures that help bring greater awareness into the world when there is receptivity. These structures are reflected in Christianity, Buddhism, Islam, and the Gita. The Bhagavad Gita is an energetic structure that when evoked brings down forces that assist a sincere seeker on his or her journey. The Gita is a summary of an ancient tradition of spiritual wisdom that has been around for thousands of years.

The Bhagavad Gita is a compelling story that describes the twists and turns of our journey back to the original purity of what we are. It is a scripture based on revelations seen by ancient Indian rishis about the nature of reality. It was recorded through the oral tradition of chanting and carried from generation to generation through teaching select young boys the verses that held this knowledge. This rich, deep, and profound body of experience was kept alive in this way until mankind's consciousness was ready for written language. To this day the Gita is kept intact through rote memorization and chanting. It was translated into Sanskrit somewhere around 1500 BCE and into English in the early 1800s.

The Gita Reveals Itself to Me

When I went to India I learned about the Gita from my teacher, who learned to chant it as a child from his grandfather who was a Brahmin priest. I struggled to understand this mythological story with my Western mind, and for a long time it was just words to me. But at some point it opened and I tapped into its rich transmission, this huge body of wisdom that proved in time to be an accurate description of the journey that I was unwittingly on. It describes a natural unfolding of stages of a journey we are all on whether we know it or not, a potentiality that lies inherent in the collective consciousness.

As time went on I discovered the ability to experience the Gita directly, as a confirmation of my own realizations. I would say, "I know that, I recognize that experience." And while this was happening there were parts that I didn't yet know, the experience had not yet come. Later I would see that it perfectly described something that had just happened. Only then could I recognize what the Gita was describing. So the Gita revealed and confirmed my experience, laying out an eternal path. It was quite a revelation. I was in awe that this spontaneous journey I was traveling on had been described thousands of years ago, in such detail. No one can see a teacher until something of the teacher is within them. No one can recognize the Bhagavad Gita for what it truly is until there is something of the Krishna or the Gita within them that can recognize it.

Along the way I got to meet Krishna, the personification of the principle described in the Gita as the manifestation of the Supreme Being. These meetings would come mostly through my teacher, Sri Atmananda. I would see Krishna in my teacher in very tangible ways showing up in the personality of my teacher. Something of Krishna was present as He spoke through my teacher—that quality of the Supreme Being embodied with a magnificent presence and authority and power—a huge tangible transmission of an inexplicable force that was both loving and true. In the early days of my time in India it was always a shock to meet this force.

I am indebted to Sri Atmananda for having demonstrated what I was engaged in and for giving me clarity when I didn't know what it was that I was experiencing. I have been able to put what has happened spontaneously and naturally to me into a structure and contemporary language as a model for others, showing the stages of the journey of consciousness and offering a detailed elaboration of the final stage that is found in the Bhagavad Gita. This can give you a perspective of where you are in the story, where you are in your own journey.

EMPOWERED BY A LIVING TEACHER

The power of the Gita is strengthened through a living teacher who is using the Gita as his or her structure for teaching. The consciousness of the teacher empowers the Gita—turns it on. People who link with that teacher access the universal energies of the Gita through the grace of the teacher empowering that scripture. Although what happened to me was spontaneous and natural, the articulation of the specific stages of that unfolding all came through my teacher and his version of the Bhagavad Gita. It gave me a large enough framework to contextualize my experiences.

This is now happening to me: When those linked with me study the Gita, they begin to build a direct connection to this universal archetypal force. It descends and empowers the quality of consciousness that they are. It is not a dogma or a religion. It is in fact a living truth, a description of what happens for every evolving soul on his or her return journey.

Studying the Gita, writing the Gita, and sharing your insights is one way that I can nurture each soul linked with me directly or indirectly without my having to be physically present. The very essence of what I am can come to you through this little book. Nothing else is required to grow that divine principle within you except sincerity and aspiration. If you have that, and if you have a modality like the Gita that truly works, then wherever you are you will be nurtured on your own journey, your own unfolding. So, in this way, the Bhagavad Gita is one of the great pillars of mankind's body of wisdom.

THE RETURN JOURNEY

This last leg of the journey of consciousness, the return journey, is where the Bhagavad Gita begins. It is a natural process, something we all go through whether we are aware of it or not. It has a beginning, a middle, and an end in the same way that a seed planted in the ground first has to emerge from the seed as a root, striving without knowing it is striving in the darkness and the mud, until the shoot breaks through the surface and then experiences the dimension of air and sun and warmth, and a whole new paradigm opens up. We are all in a maturation process. We are all seeds that have sent out shoots and have been growing over lifetimes, maturing and developing.

The Gita maps this last stage of the journey of consciousness. We are all consciousness. We are not our personalities. We are not who we think we are. We are not our story. We are not our memory. We are not our body. We are not our moods or feelings or thoughts. Those are only a by-product of us as consciousness having gotten tangled up with matter. We are all born into life in the middle of things. We are born in the middle of family and culture and circumstance. Our parents are not enlightened; they don't know who they are. We come out of childhood taking everything for granted, not knowing what it is we are taking for granted because we didn't know anything else. So we walk into life in the middle of a story.

During the return journey this entanglement of you as consciousness becomes disentangled over time, and recover what you always were. We quit struggling to be on the surface of life. We quit treading water. Finally exhausted, we start falling back into our original nature. But the ego fears this process; it keeps struggling because it only knows itself when it is on the surface. As it starts descending into the lesser-known parts of itself, it is afraid that it will die. So this journey can also be seen as a process of descending, of letting go, and falling back into our original condition. The return journey has a number of stages.

The Stages of the Bhagavad Gita

The Gita describes each stage of the final leg of the spiritual journey toward awakening as a shift in perspective, a fundamental change in one's reality. This shift happens as we learn to respond effectively to the lessons life is continuously providing: to make the necessary sacrifices, to be dogged, to be determined, to move forward with what we know to be true. In the process our conditioned inherited patterns are shed. These shifts are signs that we are tapping into the foundational source of being. The Universe is always working to manifest itself through each of us. It shows what needs to be seen and gives us the clarity and strength to meet the lessons as they arise.

The Gita is divided into three major segments. Chapters 1 through 6 deal with the struggle of the individual identity separating itself from its own personal issues—a movement from the individual personal into the individual impersonal. It involves a stepping out of taking everything personally, stepping back and developing some ability to witness. The first six chapters take us to a state of the being, or the Self. We engage in a process aimed at becoming stable in the knowing that we are not our thoughts, rather we are that which has thoughts; we are not our feelings, we are that which has feelings; we are not our body, we are that which has a body.

The second stage, described in Chapters 7 through 12, is when consciousness begins to merge with the universal principles of itself. We begin to experience more universal domains, more shared archetypal structures of the formation of consciousness, of which as individuals we only have a piece. We move into the individual universal. We begin to have a greater sense that we are a reflection of the whole, a piece of the whole. Our anger, our fear, our need to be right, our hatred, our love is shared by everyone.

As you descend into the subconscious you begin to experience this; you get in touch with the fact that everything is not so much mine, as that I am connected to everybody else who is also unconsciously connected to me. As we merge into the universal principles, much bigger forces start working in our system. Our human vehicle has to be transformed, expanded, made more capable of absorbing and accepting these increased energies and experiences that come when we move out of our individual identification into our universal identification. We eventually wake up to consciousness no longer as an individual, but as consciousness that exists everywhere all at once. This is the state of Oneness.

How we experience this process of moving from the individual toward the universal depends on whether our nature is more mental, which includes spaciousness and awareness, or more feeling, which includes the body and the heart. A more mental nature will meet itself as the universal impersonal, the vast unlimited awareness. A more feeling nature will meet itself as the universal personal, what we could call God.

In either case, we step out of our individual identity into our universal identity. It is as if the identity reaches a point where instead of saying "I am a body with a spirit," it says "I am a spirit with a body." Your individual consciousness has merged into the ocean. The drop has merged into the ocean yet comes out. But this sense that I am the ocean and I am not what comes out gets stronger and stronger until that sense of self is very broad, very expanded, not personal—impersonal in its knowing of itself as the All. This can be known in your awareness or felt as an experience. You can know it as clear insights, revelations, recognitions, and realizations in your awareness or feel it as extraordinary powerful experiences in your body. For the awareness-being that realization says, "I am Truth"; for the experiential-being that realization says, "I am God." Of course we are both, but one tends to predominate in each person.

Chapters 13 through 18 represent the final stage of the journey. At first there is a process of integration of the awakened individual with the universal states of being. One then becomes a channel and/or an instrument for the universe to manifest Itself both through us and as us. That point culminates in Chapter 15, called Purushottama Yoga, The Yoga of the Supreme Being. In this state, one becomes capable of shifting the collective consciousness from the inside out. The final three chapters of the Gita direct the divine person toward the nature of manifestation, the "work" that is now possible. One is shown the aspects of the collective unconsciousness that is obscured and which resists its evolutionary purpose. The universe becomes us and is now able to enjoy its creation.

The state when consciousness merges with its origin is utterly indescribable. Most souls end their journey there. A few will come back into the world to manifest that complete integral wisdom into their personality, body, emotions, and mind. These are the great teachers. From that place of absolute truth they recover their ability over time to descend back into the world and act as a personal individual while concurrently remaining universal and impersonal. They integrate all the experiences and openings that have occurred in their consciousness, making it real, making it lived. And then their body becomes a portal for universal forces to work through their individual form.

You who travel on this journey carry much more force, consciousness, love, knowledge, and presence than ordinary human beings. Once the journey has begun you become a radiation of consciousness of truth and oneness. You become a channel for that force of consciousness. This always expresses itself as what is real, as the state of truth and love. The Hindu word for this is *satchitananda*, truth, consciousness, and love. It is the manifesting force of existence. When you tap into this current you disengage from your identification with matter, and in the process this current flows freely and powerfully through you. The current of satchitananda is the source of all spiritual experiences that occur as it moves us to a place that is beyond all experience. In this way, step by step, the Universe manifests Itself as us.

Journey to the Self:
An Overview of Chapters 1–6

The first six chapters of the Bhagavad Gita travel about halfway along the ascending journey of consciousness to our origin. They take us to the point of no return—where we come to know the Self, when consciousness reaches sufficient velocity and distance to transcend the gravity of the human condition. The individual, through effort, is now prepared for the next stage of evolution. It takes time. The first six chapters describe the journey to that point in detail.

They introduce the concept of yoga. Yoga is the conscious and willful action we take toward a purpose: to merge with the goal, to complete what we are striving for, to realize the Self or the Soul. Yoga has six aspects: the Yoga of Dejection, the Yoga of Discrimination, the Yoga of Action, the Yoga of Knowledge, the Yoga of Renunciation, and the Yoga of Meditation.

All are interrelated. They cycle continually. The basic teaching is the same: moving the consciousness out of its identification with the human condition into identification with the spiritual condition; moving out of identification with a separate egoic existence into a relationship with an overall field of consciousness of which we are each an expression.

Yoga is an unveiling. It requires a sense of the goal. It requires persistence. At times it requires effort, while at other times it is a natural movement. These first six chapters are the effort part. It doesn't come naturally. Being a human being comes naturally. Enjoying ourselves, indulging our whims and our moods and getting what we want comes naturally. This is the habitual human condition.

The first chapter in the Gita is *The Yoga of Dejection*. The identification of consciousness with matter grows weak until it begins to disengage. This is a turbulent period. At this point of transition, the soul—the consciousness associated with a body—becomes aware of its bondage, but in a visceral, below the surface awareness. It is a turbulence going on deep in the vibration of consciousness itself, so it is hard to know what is going on. Consciousness is trying to separate from its identity with matter.

In *The Yoga of Discrimination*, the second chapter, we begin to wake up from our dejection. We begin to see what binds us and what doesn't, what frees us and what holds us back. The Yoga of Discrimination takes us to a place where we begin to understand the distinction between who we *are* as a personality, and who we are as that which *has* a personality. Discrimination helps us to understand the nature of dejection, to understand the nature of our condition, and to begin to take actions that extricate us.

The Yoga of Action, the third chapter, begins a process of inquiry. What actions take me away from my identification with the bondage that I have been suffering? What actions take me toward what I am? We start finding ways to make a distinction between the outer personality and the inner being. This process includes inquiry, spiritual practices, talking with others on the journey, and being exposed to people whose radiant presence can enhance the experience of our own presence. The more one takes action, the more the discrimination becomes strong; the stronger the discrimination, the less dejection and suffering one goes through. Discriminative action reveals knowledge—the recognition of what is real and what is not real.

Discriminative action is further explored in the fourth chapter, *The Yoga of Knowledge*—always knowledge of the truth of our Self, of what is real. With true knowledge comes the first taste of freedom, the freedom to escape the pit of bondage. True knowledge is the ability to experience, to have glimpses, to know that which we are without a personality, without a story, a mind, emotions, beliefs, or attachments. True knowledge provides the ability to build a sense of who we are outside of that conditioning. The truth gets stronger and stronger. We begin to lose the pull of the world: the habits, addictions, negativities, and the behaviors that have formed an individual identity. The conditioned human state of consciousness has a signed certificate of expiration.

When knowledge comes to a certain point, we begin to step out of the habit of the old personality and enter into the fifth chapter, *The Yoga of Renunciation*. Interest in childhood toys and the things that kept our immature state of consciousness entertained fall away. The falling away is a sign of the maturation of these first four stages of dejection, discrimination, action, and knowledge. The more conscious the renunciation, the easier it gets. We come out of the "who" we are and become more of the "what" we are. Renunciation further reinforces the earlier stages of discrimination, right action, and knowledge. Eventually renunciation becomes natural because it brings us back to what is real in us, rather than what has been programmed or conditioned.

When each of these previous five stages reaches a certain threshold, we slip gracefully into *The Yoga of Meditation*, the sixth chapter. Then we find that which lives us. That which we essentially are starts coming forward into the outer personality, causing it to grow quieter. The emerging being is always accompanied by a quieting. Things become still, settled, present. Left behind is the frantic restlessness, the treading of water.

Our lives begin to sink into the life-giving ocean of stillness that we actually are. This is meditation.

With the coming of natural meditation comes also an enhanced effectiveness in all the previous stages. Our ability to move through our dejection, our ability to discriminate, our ability to take right action, our ability to have a direct experience—knowledge—of what we are and what that means, and the falling away of the patterns of our lives that kept us in our outer personality—all are enhanced. This is why I put so much emphasis on meditation. All the previous activities require process and effort. With the coming of natural meditation, so much more can be done to bring everything else forward.

Everybody has their different capacities relative to their abilities to make progress, but these first five yogas—dejection, discrimination, action, knowledge, and renunciation—are the foundational processes that we will cycle through forever. But each time we cycle through, we are at a different vibrational frequency from before. We start this journey at one point of dismantling the habit of ourselves; then we shift to the next point until that point is complete; then we shift to the next point, and so on. This cycling is necessary even after we have become grounded in the truth of what we are, because when we reenter into matter, the world tries to coat us again. We have to continuously apply our discrimination, take actions that support this truth of what we are, periodically practice renunciation, and get back in touch with what we are through knowledge.

Throughout the entire journey we have to learn to control the senses. We falsely believe that what we, what we touch, what we taste, what we smell, and what we hear are real and give us the truth about the nature of the world and thereby who we are in the world. We believe our feelings and thoughts to be true. We are, therefore, caught up in endless inner ruminations. This is where we lose ourselves. Sense-control provides the ability to manage the human tendency to have things or to avoid things. But it is not just sensory control; it is control of the parts of ourselves that believe our own story, accept our feelings as true, or our moods as meaningful.

For most people these first six chapters take many years, even lifetimes; learning to detach from the personal self and discover the individual impersonal self can be laborious and difficult, with many traps and distractions that prevent one from coming to our true Self, the central being. But once this is attained there arises the ability to step back, to be less attached to what others say, or to getting our way, or to how things turn out. We move out of the human condition into our true nature. As we move into relationship with our inner Self, with that which lives our life, we are no longer lost in those things. This is the point of no return. We have exceeded the pull of human identity. We are no longer lost to ourselves.

These first six chapters include almost everything that we have learned in almost all traditions—the individual coming to a state that could be called individual liberation, the liberation from being a person to being consciousness—although it may not necessarily be well integrated. Ninety-five percent of seekers are in this process of becoming stable in the Self. Of that 95 percent there is probably another 20 percent who have glimpses of the next stages of the journey. These glimpses come and go, rare experiences of the journey that can come and then be completely forgotten for lifetimes before they come again. What is more common is to become stable in the Self—the state where your identity as your self as matter has switched to that of your Self as spirit. Many people are very fulfilled to complete this much. It's no small feat.

When I was revealing the first six chapters of the Gita, I was taking a station at the level of consciousness that would approximate the consciousness of a seeker at that stage of the journey. I was consciously managing the frequency I was speaking from so that this progressive revelation of the nature of the journey was proportional to the seeker's ability to match. As you read each chapter, your consciousness is being organized. A scaffolding is being built that will allow you to travel through the frequencies of consciousness that are being pointed to. Over time, this progressive realization will be there to let you know not to stop when you come to any one station, but rather to keep growing, keep moving to the next station, until the full expression of divinity finds itself in you.

The Bhagavad Gita

Chapter 1

The Yoga of Arjuna's Dejection

True dejection is a fundamental recognition that it is all a lie.
⟳ Sat Shree

The Bhagavad Gita is a very human story about a warrior, Arjuna, at the start of battle. His charioteer, Krishna, is at his side. Arjuna is the seeker. Krishna is the divine guidance that exists within each of us.

The scene opens upon a battlefield in which the mighty forces of the Kaurava family are arrayed against the equally imposing forces of the Pandava family. Dhritarashtra, the blind king of the Kauravas, is asking Sanjaya, who has the ability to see all, to tell him how the war is proceeding. The Pandavas include Arjuna and his brothers, who have come to take back the kingdom from Dhritarashtra, who would bequeath it to his son Duryodhana, even though the crown rightfully belongs to Arjuna's brother Yudhishthira. (See Appendix II for the list of main characters and their qualities.)

The Epic Battle

This epic battle is an allegory between the dark and light forces within each of us. The dark forces—the Kauravas—are those associated with what I call the error of evolution. Evolution is a process of trial and error in which material vehicles evolve to sustain consciousness. Many species came and went in the eons in which a human body and a human system developed. So we are born into a human body that is a by-product of an evolutionary process, a process that was part of the Original Intent of creation.

When we wake up in a body we are very much identified as a body, with emotions, thoughts, memories, experiences, preferences, attractions, and repulsions. When consciousness begins to awaken, it has to move beyond that identification. Consciousness either returns to itself in a movement toward light, truth, goodness, and love, or moves counter to that, in a movement toward darkness and ignorance, comfort and pleasure, following the habits of the body and the mechanisms of survival and success. These are the two forces the Bhagavad Gita is pointing to.

Although described as an outer battle, the struggle is really between our old habit of who we thought we were and a new state of being that has yet to become fully conscious. It can be a very torturous battle, especially at first. The awakening process described in the first chapter is not merely occurring on the mental plane, the emotional plane, or even the physical plane. It is occurring at the soul level, the level of consciousness. The soul can no longer remain held down in matter. Spirit can no longer believe in matter or tolerate being bound to it.

DEJECTION

Dejection occurs when the soul, the consciousness, the core quality that we are, wakes up to its state of bondage. It becomes aware of its inability to find fulfillment as usual. It becomes aware of its limitations and so experiences suffering. It longs for something else, something truer, greater, higher, even though the mind, emotions, and body may not be aware

THE BHAGAVAD GITA REVEALED

of it. This longing can create a shift in consciousness, a moment of awakening, a shift that sets a process in motion. Like a caterpillar ready to become a butterfly, dejection is the beginning of a natural process. Knowing the cause of your discomfort allows you to collaborate with it.

Understanding the Gita, even just intellectually, will assist you in working with this process that has already started. Everyone reading this book has gone or is going through this. Dejection is not a one-time deal. It happens again and again on the spiritual path. Arising in fits and starts, it tries to awaken and then collapses. Like waking up from a deep sleep, one is so torpid and taken over by slumber that waking up can be a struggle. Coming out of dejection is a similar process.

Dejection is an emerging from a lesser state of consciousness to a higher one. It happens even for non-seekers. Many people are in dejection and don't know it. They think it is just a bad mood or a bad day. That is pretty much how dejection shows up: You can't keep the harmony with your outer personality that you previously knew. There is a disturbance and you don't know why and you don't know how to fix it. Old ways don't seem to work. That is the clue.

In my experience dejection is much more pervasive than people realize. On the spiritual path it is your constant companion. It is coming and going. Your deep dissatisfaction is not due to an outward cause. There is an endless sense that something is missing, and it is not due to desire. We don't know what's wrong, just that something is wrong. We just know we want to get out of it. We don't know we are in a process of awakening. This process continues until the soul comes to the Self. When dejection occurs beyond that point, it is of a different order.

The first part of the Bhagavad Gita is about this initial emerging. The caterpillar inside the cocoon, having reached sufficient readiness, begins to dissolve in order to become a butterfly. Dejection is the beginning of dissolving. Ask the caterpillar how it feels in the cocoon, and it would probably say it's miserable. "This hurts. I don't want to do this. How can I make it stop? Give me some pills. Let's get drunk. Give me some friends, another project, another job, another relationship, anything but this!" It is a state of dis-ease. Ignorance does not like to wake up. It is a state of not knowing you don't know. Waking up from ignorance is the beginning of learning that you don't know, usually by thinking you know and then finding out that you don't. This process disengages consciousness from its previous state. It can be very stressful.

Let's begin with the first verse in Chapter 1, The Yoga of Arjuna's Dejection (Arjuna Vishada Yoga).

Dhritarashtra said:

1. *Tell me, Sanjaya, what did my sons and those of Pandu do after gathering at the field of Kuru, the field of Dharma?*

This first verse set the place and circumstance. It describes the field of Kuru, the field of dharma. This is the field of action, of engagement, of struggle and effort—the field of trying. The field of dharma means that it is through this action that the true path is discovered. It is through struggle, effort, and ordeal that how we are to live, how we are to be, and how we are to collaborate with this process becomes apparent to us. This is the context for the revelation of the Gita.

Without struggle and effort nothing changes. When it is all good and smooth and easy, when everything is going well, then we are not growing, we are not disengaging, and we are not evolving. We are in a zone in which the current sense of self that we call ego is comfortable. There is sufficient understanding, skill, and capacity from previous effort to move with our current circumstances smoothly. That is why we seem comfortable. These are the periods in which many people try to stay for their whole lives, avoiding any pain or suffering if possible. As soon as it starts hurting, we struggle to make it better. We think that the solution to life is an idea of happiness—which isn't true happiness. It is a temporary pause in the battle where we try to avoid anything that would remind us that we are, in fact, in a battle where what is at stake is our very soul. Instead we stay asleep, clinging to those things around us that make us feel safe and comfortable. We try to stay secure and avoid change.

Sorry, but life doesn't work like that. It didn't work like that in the evolution of animal life. There was striving, avoiding being eaten, and eating to survive. Every day was uncertain. A good day for a lizard is to get home without being eaten. It is a dog-eat-dog reality. Look at nature: It is bestial and cruel. At any moment anyone could die or be harmed or diminished in ways we can't imagine. We put this fact away from ourselves. We pretend it is not there. We build houses, create societies and governments and ideas about who we are and how the world is so we don't have to be present with this ultimate vulnerability that identification with a body creates.

Bodies get born, live, grow old, and die. So you might say life is a terminal disease, and we pretend it is not. We don't even want to have this conversation or be reminded of our vulnerability, our temporal existence, and the death sentence we each carry. We pretend we don't die. We strive to avoid effort, yet effort is the only way to evolve. This is true in nature and true in each human being.

The Natural Evolutionary Process

Every human being is engaged in a natural evolutionary process. We are dreaming if we think that evolution isn't continuing. It's not realistic to think there is a whole different paradigm when you die than the one that has brought you to your death. It is all part of the same movement. Ask a shoot that has just emerged from a seed, "What's the world?" It will reply, "It's dark, it's dirty, it's muddy. I don't know anything. It's a lot of effort. I hit stones and rocks and I don't know where I am going." It is struggle and effort. Only when it has broken through the surface does it become aware of a completely different paradigm.

The plant doesn't have a human mind, so it doesn't resist the next stage in which it grows stronger, puts out leaves and matures, and is vulnerable to wind and animals. It doesn't resist in the way humans resist change. That is the curse of self-awareness. We keep thinking it could or should be different. We don't understand the necessity for change and growth. Instead we constantly seek to resist or control things to prevent change. We thus create blockages to our own natural evolution, blockages which inevitably bring pain and suffering. We attribute that pain and suffering to causes other than our own choices. We attribute the cause of our pain onto people in our lives, to our circumstances, to our current state of health, or to the weather, rather than to know we are the cause of our own misery simply by not living aligned with this primal evolutionary need for change and growth.

We can go smoothly or we can go kicking and screaming. But the torrent of this evolutionary impulse is going to force us to change and grow, whether we like it or not. There is a lot less pain when we quit resisting. When we stay invested in the old ways and maintain the position of who we are with our stories about how the world is or should be—then we suffer. When we are invested in these things, we accept or create a story that rationalizes and justifies why we don't change and grow. This becomes our belief, opinion, perspective, or point of view—the lens through which we view the world. When someone questions our belief or our story, it is an act of war. "Who do you think you are?" Or "How dare you!" Or we feel overtaken by someone's questioning and become lost, confused, or crushed.

The Gita offers a true allegory of this process. We are all in the midst of a battlefield, even if our minds think things are good now. "I have a house and money, I am protected, they can't get me here." This will last only for a while. You will not survive this journey. Who you think you are as an ego will not survive, just as the ego of a young child cannot survive when it leaves the sandbox behind. Again and again we have to leave our previous identity behind as we grow older. This is a turbulent process. Here the Gita speaks of the battle of emerging from a previous paradigm—a previous way of seeing the world and yourself—into a new way that is not yet formed, not yet articulated.

THE OPPOSING FORCES

Sanjaya said:

2. *Seeing the army of the Pandavas arrayed for battle, King Duryodhana approached his teacher Drona and spoke thus:*
3. *O Master! Behold this vast army of the Pandavas. Your talented pupil, Drupada's son, has marshaled this army for the battle.*
4. *In this army there are mighty heroes and archers like Yuyudhana, Virata, and Drupada. Each of them can be compared with Bhima and Arjuna in battle.*
5. *Dhrishtaketu, Chekitana, the valiant king of Kashi, Purujit, Kuntibhoja, and Shaibya, the best among men, are also there . . .*
7. *O best among the twice-born, I will now tell you the names of our distinguished generals.*
8. *Foremost amongst us are thyself, Bhisma, Karna, also Kripa, the ever victorious in battle, and there are others like Ahswatthama, Vikarna, and the son of Somadatta.*

Who is standing in this battlefield? The Kauravas represent the forces of darkness, denial, resistance, and opposition. I call these the forces of inertia. They resist change and attempt to exert control and dominate. These forces pervade all human dynamics. They distort our ability to know and experience reality as it is.

The Pandavas represent the forces of light, cooperation, tolerance, and harmony. Those who are like the Pandavas have learned how to cooperate with the need for change and growth. They represent the happier, more harmonious, and successful human beings. When the soul's development of consciousness has reached this stage of the journey, it is more open to the new, to change. It is more aware and inquiring. This is not an ordinary human being drinking beer, dimly looking out at life, watching TV, having kids and getting through the days pretending they are not going to die. It's not like that anymore. One is alert. One asks, "How do I live, how do I be, what is the purpose of this whole thing?" A quest has begun. We try to find what is real and true. We develop our minds. We discover how to stop taking actions that create pain; we start taking actions that create more happiness, cooperation, and understanding.

The human intelligence has now reached a certain stage of maturity—a mental capacity, an understanding of the nature of the world and how to function in it, a wisdom of the heart which has become more and more open and capable of seeing the truth of things. These are signs that the soul has matured. That which has kept us contracted begins to relax; that which has kept us locked in our identification with matter begins to loosen its hold.

One may still be unaware of the spiritual path but is just beginning to feel better about life as it is. One discovers that when sitting in nature there is greater happiness than when striving for control. Such a person reads about the higher possibilities of consciousness, about cooperation, and becomes uplifted and inspired to get involved, to make the world a better place. In the process we open up to a sense of purpose beyond our little egos, our family, community, religion, and country. We become more and more expanded. Even though the ego is still identified, "I am a Democrat, I am a Republican," it is still in a larger context than the individual ego at home with the kids, the spouse, and the job.

With the broadening of this awareness one begins to tap in to a shift that is happening in the collective consciousness. One becomes more engaged in a new expanded awareness. "I am going to fight for the good." One takes a position from a broader point of view and becomes more responsible. As one becomes more able to respond, one grows into a new way of being, a new paradigm. As one takes on these expanded responsibilities, they become more and more established in a new aligned awareness. This becomes the basis for the next paradigm to open up. Throughout the ages this is how human beings evolved from little tribes to villages to medieval city-states to modern cities and countries, to the ability to print and invent and create commerce. This is how we got to where we are now.

This is what the Pandavas represent—those who have reached a stage of maturity in their human identification. They feel they can make a difference. They participate. They start taking on causes. They start looking to be a good person, to have integrity, to keep promises, to do the right thing, to stand up for truth, to protect the weak, to help those in need. They become idealists and create a sense of morals and ethics. This is human maturity.

Beyond the Human Paradigm—Turbulent and Tumultuous

These opposing forces are described in detail in the Gita. Being a better human being—even a noble and admirable human being, even a great human being—is still being a human being. The true transition, where consciousness begins to take its attention away from identification with everything around it and begins to turn its attention on its own nature, has not yet begun. By turning one's attention from who one is as a person, as one's story, as one's family and job, as one's thoughts and ideas of the world, and starting to turn one's attention inward, one becomes more and more aware of what it is that assigns value and identity. This process is a struggle and takes effort.

These first verses set the stage for the Gita. They let us know that this is not just about happiness and harmony and cooperation, how to get along with people and feel good. It's about a struggle to move into the correct relationship with what is actually true, lasting, and eternal—true even beyond the human paradigm, even beyond human relationships.

From the vantage point of what it feels like, we could say dejection feels like shit. To give you a clue, dejection always thinks it is too much. It thinks it can't do it. It thinks it is impossible to bear because it is so habituated to being small. It doesn't know how to be large. It thinks it can't be large. It has to make itself large. It has to make itself different. But in fact it is a natural process. It is something we surrender to, not something we do. So the nature of dejection is that we experience our vulnerability. We experience being outside our comfort zone. We experience being overtaken, but we don't know why.

Now let's come back to the Bhagavad Gita and pick up where we left off.

10. *This huge army of ours under the command of Bhishma is quite strong, while the other side led by Bhima also appears to be adequate.*

11. *Therefore, all of you remaining in your respective positions must protect Bhishma on all sides and on all fronts.*

12. *At this juncture, Bhishma, the great grandfather of the Kurus, blew his conch to cheer up Duryodhana. The sound of the conch was like the roaring of a lion.*

13. *All of a sudden, conches, kettledrums, tabors, drums, and cow horns blared forth simultaneously, making a tumultuous sound.*

14. *Then, seated in the magnificent chariot drawn by white horses, Sri Krishna and Arjuna blew their celestial conches . . .*

19. *The tumultuous sound echoing through heaven and earth rent the hearts of Dhritarashtra's sons.*

Consciousness awakening within matter is tumultuous. It is an acceleration of what was stuck in dejection. Suddenly the whole system is becoming activated. We are in a crisis. This is the awakening of spiritual energy in the body. The entire system is electrified with a sense of peril, a sense of necessity, a sense of something coming. The process is very turbulent. These verses describe it perfectly. The unconscious parts of ourselves—the ego and the habitual parts of ourselves—are most disturbed by this awakening. But the parts of us that are aligned with truth become enlivened, motivated, and capable.

Our capacity for action, our capacity to meet what is binding us, comes forward. Prior to that we were still victims. It is very difficult to wake up to the realization that you have a say about how miserable, bound, and stuck you've been feeling. This is the beginning of waking up as the authority of your own life, to choose what is arising. This is the beginning of the struggle to separate the untruth of you from the truth of you. Because this rising force is not from the ego, not from the habitual part of you, but draws its strength from truth and consciousness itself, it can be very disturbing.

My first awakening went relatively smoothly, but I discovered this is not always the case. I discovered a website called "*kundalini* emergency" that described symptoms of people who were having a perilous awakening. There were panic attacks, physical pain, breathing problems, sleeplessness, and endless restlessness and discomfort. These were all symptomatic of this spiritual force of consciousness rising up in the individual system, pushing its way to the surface through layers of resistance, fear, and obscurity.

With the awakening, perhaps for the first time, one may experience the force of consciousness within oneself. This is a startling experience initially. One may feel a much more expanded capacity for presence or love, as if cast into a whole other dimension of being, given a glimpse of the gods or the heavens. These would be signs that, at least for that moment, the force of awakening consciousness has a free channel to your surface self. You could experience something of that expanded awareness. But for the most part, most people will go back into the turbulence, back into the process.

This awakening of consciousness is the beginning of an internal transformation process, but at this stage we have no discrimination. We don't know what is going on, we feel like the victim, and we tend to take it very personally. If it was a great experience, you may feel exalted and think you are God—you found it and you are the one! Your ego will take over and proclaim itself as a realized being until someone catches on. But inevitably the ego will convert it into its own thing, and you will fall back into a diminished state of consciousness. Then dejection will be even more poignant, but also the discrimination improves. You say, "I guess that wasn't really it."

When I had my first awakening experience, it quieted the next day. I chalked it up as one of those Maslow peak experiences—what the psychologist Abraham Maslow described as an unforgettable epiphany that happens not just to mystics, but also to ordinary people. "That was interesting." And I went about my day. My attitude toward these things was that they come and go, which was helpful. I knew it didn't mean anything more than what had happened. It was a beautiful glimpse, but I didn't have a clue as to what to do about it, or what it meant, or how to put it into action. So I let it go. I did not know what had actually happened then. The discrimination had not come yet.

20. *Seeing the sons of Dhritarashtra ready for the battle, Arjuna raised his bow,*
21. *And said to Sri Krishna, "Please place my chariot in the middle of the two armies,*
22. *And keep it there until I have surveyed these warriors who have assembled for battle and have found out with whom I will have to fight."*
23. *Let me scan all the well-wishers of the evil-minded son of Dhritarashtra who have assembled here to fight.*

Arjuna is feeling his oats, he's feeling jazzed. He is feeling like, "I can do this. This looks good. I'm the one. Show me who I am here to kill. Show me how can I convert this into something that will serve my ego."

Arjuna's "Oh Shit!" Moment

Sanjaya said:

24. *O King, being thus addressed by Arjuna, Sri Krishna placed the magnificent chariot in the middle of both armies,*
25. *In front of Bhishma, Drona and the other kings and said, "Partha, behold all these opposing armies of the Kurus assembled here."*
26. *Arjuna saw fathers, grandfathers, teachers, maternal uncles, brothers, sons, grandsons and friends all standing there ready to fight . . .*
28. *Seeing all the relatives and friends standing on the battlefield eager to fight, he was filled with deep remorse and with sadness spoke thus:*

Arjuna said:

29. *Krishna, seeing these relatives arrayed for battle, my limbs give way, my mouth is parched, my body trembles, and my hairs stand on end.*
30. *The bow Gandiva is slipping from my hands and my skin is burning. I am unable to stand and my head is reeling.*
31. *And, Keshava, I am seeing inauspicious omens and find no good in killing my kinsmen in this battle.*

In this paralyzing moment Arjuna cried, "Oh shit, what am I up against?" Notice who allowed Arjuna to come to that "Oh, shit" moment: Krishna, who drove the chariot between the two armies. The divine in Arjuna was the one who allowed him to see what it was that this was heralding. Arjuna had a glimpse of his ego. He had the first glimpse of how vested he was because of his attachments to his kinsmen.

The Kauravas represent all of our human limitations, all of our human ideas of ourselves from the lowest to the highest. These are our various qualities of human nature: envy, jealousy, pride, the need to control and dominate and be right. It is also our sense of good, worth, value, and meaning, as well as our sense of worthlessness, powerlessness, and meaninglessness. It is all these things we have believed to be true. Some are qualities we are very attached to, that have been critical to our sense of self-worth, who we are in the world and what other people think of us. Some of them are obstacles, barriers, and veils. In this moment, for a brief instant, Arjuna saw the problem.

Unlike early dejection where we don't know what is happening, now the activation of the spiritual energy is pushing up issues to surface consciousness. Arjuna is beginning to experience, as the seeker, the nature of what it is that is before him, even before his mind has discrimination or mental clarity. He just knows he feels awful. He just knows that this is wrong.

And who is saying it's wrong? Ego. Ego has its own harmony. Ego has come to this point by getting all its conflicting aspects to collaborate together. When this force comes in, it is a disturbance right down in the fundamental structure of our identity. And it just feels wrong. What do we do with this wrong feeling? We try to make it go away. We take medications, we get treatment, we get drunk or get laid, anything but to be with this. In this case Arjuna does this by rationalizing and justifying why he shouldn't continue.

Arjuna Rationalizes and Justifies

32. *Krishna, I am not desirous of victory or kingdom or pleasures; what is the use of all this happiness or even life to us?*
33. *Those for whose sake we desire kingship, happiness and pleasure are all arrayed here risking their lives and wealth.*
34. *Teachers, fathers, sons and grandsons, maternal uncles, fathers-in-law, brothers-in-law, and all other relatives are here.*
35. *Krishna, I do not want to kill them even if the are ready to kill me; not to speak of the gains on earth, even the lordship over the three worlds will not prompt me to kill them.*

In these verses Arjuna is trying to convince himself not to fight. If you look at the nature of rationalization and justification, it is to convince ourselves not to take the required action. There are multiple aspects to this allegory. One is what the mind does when awakening happens. It tries to find a rationalization or justification for why it is occurring. It tries to make it stop so we can feel better. It is total ignorance. We don't know what is going on, so we treat it as if it were a physical or psychological problem. But in this case, there is another way to look at it. What is making it impossible for Arjuna to go forward is his attachment, his misplaced compassion, his affection and loyalty to those that came from the community he was born into. His relatives and teachers and other important people helped shape his sense of self and his positive ego so that he could become a successful man. He had a lot of positive influences in his life. He had gratitude, but he also had sentiment and attachment. The idea of destroying his kinsmen was intolerable to his surface consciousness, even though they were trying to destroy him.

In this allegory we have the struggle between dark and light, good and bad. We are attached to the things that bind us. The very nature of identity is repetition and agreement. We make something real, even if it is not real, by repeating it enough and getting enough people to agree with us. Falsehood is nothing but repetition and agreement. Politicians are very effective with this these days. It's a strategy that has existed throughout ages—repetition and agreement to convince people, to sell your beliefs, views, or products. For each of us, our relatives are the agreement for you. They are usually the ones that define your existence, that establish if you are OK or not. We become attached to these positive or negative affirmations of who we are as separate beings.

40. *When the clan is destroyed, the age-old family virtues disappear and vice takes over the entire race . . .*
45. *What a pity! We are bent upon committing such a great sin of killing our own kinsmen just for the sake of the pleasure of the crown.*

Spiritual awakening is not only the end of the dark and obscure sides of life; it is also the end of our human life, our enjoyable habits, our human comfort and security—all those little pleasures that make life worth living. When truth wakes up it doesn't care. It sees these are unimportant attachments—structures—by which we are hooked. Of course our ego is going to rationalize and justify why to keep them. We hang onto what feels good and reject what doesn't. It doesn't feel good not to have what feels good. Initially it is really difficult to collaborate with this process. It runs counter to everything our ego has been organized around—the good and the bad, the pleasurable and the unpleasurable, those who love us and those who don't, those we get along with and those we don't, our attractions and repulsions. They are all bondage.

What hooks us? Happiness hooks us. Attraction, the possibility of human love hooks us. Attention hooks us. Recognition hooks us—as well as rejection, judgment, complaint, dissatisfaction, and criticism. They all hook us. Either side of this metronome hooks us. Happiness and sorrow, pleasure and pain—this is the music we all dance to, whether we know it or not. The Gita is about ending this endless movement. It is about getting rid of the metronome.

It is a completely different thing, utterly outside of human ideas. It is not about nobility. It is not about greatness. It is not about an accomplishment, unless you consider undoing that which you want to accomplish an accomplishment. Of course Arjuna would rationalize and justify not going forward. Not only is he feeling like crap, he can't by any stretch of the imagination understand why he should destroy all these loved ones, all the things that helped form his sense of worth and who he was.

So now you are beginning to get what a "truth book" is about; you are beginning to get the truth that this book reveals. You are beginning to get a sense that we are not talking about a happy human accomplishment here. We are not talking about being a better human. We are talking about a completely different paradigm, a completely different order.

One's Worst Nightmare

This chapter now comes to its conclusion. Arjuna is overtaken by his dejection.

46. *It will be better for me if the weapon-wielding sons of Dhritarashtra kill me in this battlefield when I am unarmed and unresisting.*

Sanjaya said:

47. *Saying thus, Arjuna, whose mind was agitated by grief, threw down his bow and arrow on the battlefield and sat silently in the chariot.*

True dejection is a fundamental recognition that it is all a lie. It is very difficult for our consciousness to be present with this. It is the destruction of everything good and bad and all we hold near and dear. Arjuna is getting a glimpse of what he is doing from the point of view of his ego, his attachments, his ethics and morality, his tradition and cultural order. From his egoic perspective, he is seeing that this utter destruction is wrong, that he would rather die, that he would rather be killed and forget this awakening—go back to sleep, go back to unconsciousness, go back into not knowing. He doesn't want to experience this. He has talked himself out of it.

But it's complicated. Arjuna is a great warrior. Of the five Pandava brothers, he is the one with the celestial weapons. Yet he is saying, "I can't do this." It is a paralyzing moment in the journey of consciousness when one has come far enough along to get a glimpse of where one is headed.

It is never as horrific as the ego sees it. It is actually wonderful. But at the moment when you enter into your next stage of evolution, what you see first is the darkness, the unworkability of it, relative to what you have known. It is like trying to get a child out of the sandbox. The child doesn't know what is going to happen next. He doesn't know yet about riding bikes or playing baseball or being with his friends. He just likes his little sandbox. It is this resistance, this unwillingness to change, to let go of what we know, that keeps us stuck.

But this point on the journey is actually quite a high state. I sometimes have people come to me in that state and I am thrilled. They are telling me how awful it is, how trapped they feel, and I can't help but smile. I know it is a true glimpse, a true showing of that which is not yet known. Yes, from the vantage point of ego it looks awful, it looks like your undoing; but from the vantage point of truth, it looks like your freedom. That's why it is called the gateless gate. From the side of ego it looks like a formidable, impossible barrier. From the side of truth there is no barrier.

These moments occur along the spiritual path at regular intervals. If you are fortunate to have an authentic spiritual teacher, then the more time you spend in that presence, the more often these moments will occur, because the resisting and denying aspects of the ego can't hold up. You keep being shown the next thing you have to let go of or stop doing. Initially it looks like you can't, and that's where you stop. But learning to be in these moments and yet not to believe them is the key to going beyond dejection.

Krishna was right next to Arjuna. If he hadn't been, Arjuna probably would not have had this philosophical moment. Without the presence of Krishna he wouldn't have seen the consequences of his actions, which was to be the end of his life as he knew it. He might have gone and lived in the woods as a *sannyasi*, avoiding his relatives, hiding in caves. He would not have recovered his true self.

We can't proceed without the presence of a Krishna. We don't have sufficient light or freedom for the force to move in our system at the beginning of the journey. This is key. When the light of truth is sufficiently bright, we come out of the morass of our identification with matter and begin to recover who we are as spirit. Until then we fall back. Many, many, many people spend lifetimes and lifetimes popping out and falling back because they don't want to change, or it looks too hard. It takes something else to create sufficient momentum to push against the collective tide of the habit of ego and to begin to really reenter the path, this yoga.

The Gita is describing what really happens. It took me time to move through the story part of the Gita and get to the essence, but once I began to match my experience with understanding, I started getting it: "Oh, that is what's happening, that is what's going on in me." I started to get a glimpse of the next thing and then would retreat because my consciousness didn't know how to hold it. Each time we approach a new ceiling, it feels like non-existence to the ego. To ego it looks like the end of you. But consciousness doesn't think of death or not death. Consciousness doesn't know it either can or cannot exist. Only ego thinks of these things. Existence or non-existence is not real for consciousness, for it is both. It is existing and non-existing at the same time. The part of you that experiences terror when you have a glimpse of the truth is your ego. Your being isn't in terror. Being is what is there when the terror goes away.

What Arjuna had was a glimpse of the end of ego. But at first, truth always looks like your worst nightmare. It keeps showing up as what you don't want to experience. For Arjuna, because of the poignancy of the situation, because of the vested forces at play, he was brought to a moment of recognition. His ego just wanted to retreat and hide. That is just what he would have done had Krishna not been there. Like Arjuna, we need sufficient light to come out of our identification with matter and recover who we are as spirit. It is a process.

The next chapter describes how we develop discrimination in order to know who it is that we truly are.

CHAPTER 2

The Yoga of Discrimination

Untruth has no existence and truth never ceases to exist.
∽ VERSE 63

A t the end of the first chapter a dejected Arjuna throws his bow and arrow onto the battlefield. Dejection is an experience of bondage, but without knowing that it is bondage. The eternal being has started to come forward, but the outer personality doesn't have a clue as to what is happening. Before we grapple with the Yoga of Discrimination we need to understand the outer personality more fully.

CAGED IN THE OUTER PERSONALITY

We are imprisoned by our outer personality! Don't fool yourself. We live in our thoughts and ideas, our stories and daydreams, our memories and musings, and every one of them comes from impressions gathered in the outer sensory world through the body's five senses. If it weren't for the body and the mind that interprets the senses, you wouldn't have a daydream. You wouldn't have a story. You wouldn't have a belief structure. Just lie in an isolation tank for a few hours in a state of sensory deprivation, and you will begin to recognize how accustomed we are to living in a state of continuous stimulation. The personality is formed through interaction between our consciousness and the outer world through the body. This is the only reality an embodied consciousness knows.

The personality may know a higher thought versus a lower thought, or a higher feeling versus a lower feeling. It may know pain versus pleasure or comfort versus discomfort. But that is all within the sensory structure that is its foundation, our sense of separate self. In my experience this identification is more entrenched here in the West than in other places, probably because our educational system puts such an emphasis on mental development. We have spent so many years training the mind to navigate through this outer and inner world. We use the mind to try to come to some happy sense of self, some harmony, some balance.

The personality becomes the cage we live in. We don't even know that we are in the cage because we don't know anything else. Like a fish in water. Someone asks, "How is the water?" And of course the fish says, "Water, what water?" We are the fish living inside a fishbowl full of accumulated impressions from the interaction of the body and the outer world. These accumulated impressions go on even when we sleep. They become part of our dreams as well as our waking processes. Embodied consciousness has a huge content, both subtle and outer/physical. Everything we think and contemplate and analyze is due to this gathering of impressions.

When you wake up to the spiritual dimension, turbulence occurs within your fishbowl that doesn't seem to have an outward source. It arises from something you don't know about. It is as if somebody is shaking your bowl, and suddenly all the things that were in order are stirred up, and you don't know what is going on. When we finished Chapter 1, Arjuna was in a rigorous process of trying to reestablish his equilibrium. His bowl had been stirred, and he was trying to make it stop. He thought the cause of the stirring was the battle before him. He was faced with the possibility of the loss of all of his attachments and beliefs and morality. He rationalized and justified. So he said, "No, we are not going to do this. We are going to try to put it all back in order."

Arjuna didn't know he was doing that. He didn't have a clue. He was in dejection. Like us, then the mind kicks in with rationalizations and justifications to try to reestablish its equilibrium, to find the cause of the problem. You go to a psychiatrist. You go to a doctor or counselor. They tell you what to do; then you do those things, hoping it brings order. Sometimes it works. That's the bitch of the thing. A spiritual awakening is occurring and you don't even know it. You just think it is a bad month.

Awakening is not anything an ordinary ego would want. Let's be clear. No ego would seek what you find on the spiritual path. Due to the popularization of the spiritual path these days, the ego thinks the spiritual path is about something it wants. So it collaborates, at least at first, or until it gets hard. Then it loses interest. The Yoga of Dejection is not something the ego would want. It is, in fact, miserable. Yet it is an ongoing process, a means of union with the truth of who you are.

Whenever we live in this outer personality, we are unaware that the personality came with an expiration date. When we sign the birth certificate, we don't see the death certificate underneath. They are signed at the same time. Your birth certificate and your death certificate are concurrent. The only thing not filled in is the date. Who knows? On some plane the date is probably also there.

Here's the deal: No matter what body you have, it is going to get old and die. At some point it is going to get sick, uncomfortable, and diseased. You are going to have all kinds of things go wrong. Before it is over you are likely to wish you never had one. When you understand this, then you understand what it is, in fact, we are striving for. We are trying to find out what is real, what lasts, what it is that lives life, what it is that has a body.

Now the Gita begins to describe what you truly are, and the correct relationship with truth so that truth begins to become real for you, the person. You begin to understand, like a fish suddenly thrown out of the water, what you are experiencing. It's a momentary recognition of what you are. This moment of discrimination is actually a tangible experience in the mental or vital or physical plane of your true nature. But you don't know what it is at first; it takes time. You have to teach the outer personality. In the same way it was programmed to be an outer personality in the first place, it has to be programmed to recognize itself as truth, as consciousness. The Yoga of Discrimination takes us to a place where we begin to understand the distinction between "who" we are as a personality, versus "what" we are that has a body and a personality.

So let's go into Chapter 2, The Yoga of Discrimination (Samkhya Yoga).

Sanjaya said:

48. *To him who was thus overcome by grief, dejected and confused, and whose eyes were filled with tears, Krishna spoke thus:*

The Blessed Lord said:

49. *From where came this attachment to you at this hour of peril, Arjuna? It is not for noble souls; it will lead you neither to heaven nor to glory.*
50. *Yield not to cowardice; it is not befitting of you. Get rid of this faint-heartedness and stand up, you, the scorcher of enemies.*

Clearly Krishna's intent is to bring out what was hidden in Arjuna's nature. Arjuna had laid out in the previous chapter his perfectly justified rationalization of why he shouldn't fight. These are the first words that came out of Krishna. "Where did this come from? You are a warrior, why are you talking like some kind of philosopher? What is this whole thing you've created?" If it weren't for Krishna, Arjuna would be in the woods somewhere dodging his enemies. He's pushing Arjuna to question his assumptions so that he won't slip back into dejection.

ARJUNA'S FIRST SURRENDER

Arjuna said:

54. *I am overcome by pity and faint-heartedness. My mind is puzzled; I am unable to know what is my duty. I surrender to Thee; I am Thy disciple. Please guide me in the correct path . . .*

Sanjaya said:

56. *O King! After saying this to Sri Krishna, Arjuna, the destroyer of foes, proclaimed, "I will not fight," and became silent.*

Arjuna recognizes that he doesn't know what is going on and turns to Krishna to guide him. This is the first time that Arjuna sees that he has a problem outside of his outer personality. There is a recognition of something inside that is saying, "Krishna is right, it is not so simple. I can't just go into the woods and be happy with that." Some part of him knows that what he has just rationalized and justified isn't real. So when Krishna pointed that out, he is bewildered. He doesn't know what to do next. All his structures for explaining and rationalizing and organizing his life have just collapsed. Overcome, he says, "I don't know what to do."

This is a moment of awakening. A moment of humility. He is not being arrogant as he was when he said, "Lead me to the front of the armies and show me with whom I will have to fight." He's saying, "Oh shit, I don't know what is going on. I don't know what is happening." He has reached the third stage of knowledge. In the first stage you don't know you don't know. In the second stage you think you know but you don't—which is where Arjuna was. In the third stage you know you don't know. Arjuna has come to, "I know I don't know"—a critical transition point that takes us out of dejection. Prior to that we resist, we fight, and the outer personality still rules. But until we come to that moment of receptivity, of knowing we don't know, nothing will change. This is the first surrender in the Bhagavad Gita. Surrender, just like dejection, is a constant companion on the spiritual path, because it is only through surrender that we come out of what binds us and move to the next level. This is the role of dejection, to wake us up and show us what's next.

In the West we are so willful and independent, striving to do things our own way. It acts as a barrier to being able to step outside of ourselves and be open to change, open to new teachings. Of course there are a lot of people who would give us wrong information at that stage, and it takes grace to have the capacity to recognize true advice. It is not about just letting yourself be convinced by somebody; rather, it is a recognition in some part of your being that knows what is true.

Dejection begins to end when we surrender and recognize that we know we don't know. That moment when we cry out for God, when we cry out for help, when we cry out knowing we can no longer do it ourselves—that is the moment of surrender. It brings in grace and forces much larger than ourselves—even if the guru isn't present—that assist us in making this transition. This is a very key transition, an opening—a shift from the old paradigm to a new paradigm that you don't know yet. You don't know what this new world is that you are entering into. You don't even know it is a new world. You just know the old world doesn't work any more.

THE ETERNAL NATURE OF THE SOUL

57. *Then, O Bharata, Sri Krishna, with a smile, spoke the following words to Arjuna, who was full of sorrow.*

Dejection has humbled Arjuna. He is now capable of receiving the revelation of the Gita. Krishna speaks:

58. *Arjuna, you are speaking like a wise man but grieve over those who should not be grieved for. Wise men grieve neither for the dead nor for the living.*
59. *There was never a time when you, I, or these kings ceased to exist, nor shall there ever come a time when we will not exist.*
60. *Just as the embodied self undergoes the stages of adolescence, youth, and old age, so also it acquires another body. The wise are not deluded about this.*

Krishna smiled because Arjuna was ready to receive. Arjuna could hear it now. And Krishna began to say, *"We never cease to exist."* We are not that which has an expiration date. We are something other than that. *"Just as the embodied self undergoes the stages of adolescence, youth, and old age, so it acquires another body."* It is just a body, it is just a personality, which we inhabit for a period of time and then we drop it. So what is it that inhabits this personality? What are we if we are not our mind or thoughts or feelings or our sense of personal self?

61. *Arjuna, the feelings of heat and cold, pleasure and pain, are caused by the contact of senses with the objects of*

pleasure. These feelings are temporary and recurring in nature; therefore, endure them calmly.

62. *O best among men, the wise men who do not get perturbed with this feeling of pain and pleasure are indeed fit to attain immortality.*

When we get a sense of what we are as other than the body, then comes a capacity that is revealed in the above verses. We develop an ability to endure calmly the ups and downs, the moods and the swings, the happy moments and the sad moments, the angers and sorrows and regrets. These all are the territory of the personality; simply temporary feelings, recurring in nature. It is an art to not take them so seriously, to not take them so personally. Taking it personally and taking it seriously are the same thing. To see where you are identified, just look at what is serious for you in your life, where your issues are, where your problems are. This is a clue to know where your consciousness is still locked up. When you begin to experience the authentic truth of yourself, then you move toward a true recognition of what you are; and in that, the you who does not get perturbed with this feeling of pain and pleasure is indeed fit to attain immortality. You attain your true nature.

63. *Untruth has no existence and truth never ceases to exist. The knowers of truth have come to this conclusion after scrutinizing both these maxims.*

64. *That alone which pervades this universe is indestructible. No one has the power to destroy this imperishable substance.*

65. *Arjuna, all these bodies are perishable but not that which dwells in them; therefore, grieve not and fight . . .*

66. *It is never born nor does it die. It comes into embodiment again and again; it is birthless, eternally present and is not slain when the body is slain.*

THE BHAGAVAD GITA REVEALED

Just reading these verses can connect you to something. They point to truth. They point to the reality that you actually are, which is not dependent on your personality, your body, your story, or your memory. This is the magic of the Bhagavad Gita. It is a book that points to truth and how to move into a living relationship with it. The idea that untruth has no existence and truth never ceases to exist is the key to the Bhagavad Gita. It says that even this outer personality is not untruth, even this human identity is not untruth. They are expressions of the one truth and have their own validity. However, these expressions are temporary and reoccurring in nature. The higher truth, the one that pervades and permeates everything, is eternal and unchanging, even though outwardly it may appear to change endlessly.

This concurrent knowledge, this co-knowing of the passing and the permanent, the unsettled and the settled, the silent and the noisy, the still and the active, is the unique message of the Gita. It points not just to the unchanging truth alone; it points to the all-pervading truth as well.

But in the interim, in the first stage of this process of moving ourselves out of absolute identification with the outer personality, we have to put our attention on that which is eternal. We have to meet it, find it, and know it until it becomes as real to us as our outer personality. Then we have let go of the "who" we believe we are and become the "what" we truly are, and were always meant to be, which is truth incarnate, consciousness incarnated.

BIRTHS AND DEATHS, BIRTHS AND DEATHS

68. *Arjuna, one who knows the soul to be birthless, imperishable and eternal, how can he kill anybody or how can he be the cause for killing?*

69. *As a person changes worn-out clothes for new ones, so also the soul discards worn-out bodies and takes on new bodies . . .*

73. *And even if you think that this soul is subject to constant birth and death you still should not grieve.*

Krishna is revealing the eternal nature of the soul. The soul goes through births and deaths, births and deaths. What we are in essence is eternal. This essence is the foundation for discrimination. When you know yourself as the soul, you will know yourself as something other than the outer personality— something other than your mind and thoughts and beliefs and emotions and story. Arjuna is being introduced to the principle that what we are in truth is this eternal principle of the soul that never dies and is never born.

74. *Whosoever is born shall die and rebirth is inevitable for the dead, therefore you should not grieve over this.*
75. *Beings are unmanifest before birth and unmanifest after death. They are manifest between these two states. Then what is there to be grieved for?*

Here Krishna introduces the principle of reincarnation, the idea of the continuity of the consciousness through lifetimes after lifetimes. Just imagine if you, as you are now, never died. Suppose you, this person that is you, could live eternally. How would you live? How would you design your life? How would you organize yourself? What would be your sense of time and importance? How would the issues and the dramas and the problems that are occurring show up if you knew you were eternal and you could not die? Of course if we as our individual personalities lasted eternally, it would be another form of hell. We would grow weary of being ourselves for eternity. After a couple hundred years we'd be done. The advantage of dying is that everything is more precious because it ends. Things are more interesting. Life has more edge to it.

But reincarnation is not something we can know directly; what we can know directly is our eternal unchanging nature. Once we have a sense of what the Gita is describing here as the soul, we move in relationship to something other than the usual surface personality—other than the world that exists outside of us and our relationship to it and the stories that we create about it. We get in touch with a new reference point, like a fish outside of the water. When it is out of the water it can know something of water; but when it is in the water there is no way to know it. This is the same thing. Touching the soul gives us a vantage point, a reference point by which we can know the nature of our condition, the nature of what we truly are.

76. *Some see this as a wonder, others speak of it as a wonder, others listen to it in wonder, and there are people who are unable to understand anything even after hearing about it.*
77. *Arjuna, the soul that dwells in the body of all beings can never be slain; therefore you should not grieve for anyone.*

To know one's self as the soul is the key to discrimination. From that vantage point, when we look at our life, we can see what is really going on. In the normal course of human life we come to an understanding of ourselves as one part of our personality looking at another part of our personality. Our emotional nature can feel empathetically what is happening, even though our mental doesn't know; or our mental can understand what is going on with us, even though the emotions don't know. Within the outer personality there is feeling and understanding. This is psychology. But the knowingness that Krishna is referring to draws upon something other than the outer personality. It is not intellectual. That is why it is so difficult to explain or identify. It is not just a mental knowing. It is a knowing of your whole being of what is true and what is not true.

When through discrimination the sense of the soul has come forward, it is as if we are in a magnetic field of attraction and repulsion. We are repulsed by that which is not truth and attracted to that which is truth. Like a compass pulled to north, this sense comes to us of what is true, what is real, or what is not true, what is not real. Yet it is only a relative repulsion and a relative attraction, which can still be very much coated by the personality. But if we follow it through, we will see that even the personality, through the veils of the personal self, is trying to emerge from its entrapment. It is seeking a way to arrive at the thing it truly seeks.

Why do we seek comfort? Because when we are comfortable we can be quieter. When we are uncomfortable we are more restless. So comfort is not wrong; it brings us some relative aspect of the silence and stillness of the soul itself. Similarly with pleasure. Seeking things that are attractive, that we want, is not wrong. It is just a veiled looking for that which brings us the bliss that comes when we are with ourselves as truth. It's a veiled truth, a veiled experience of our connection with our higher possibility. Existence is bliss. This whole dimension of physical existence is bliss. We separate ourselves from the bliss because of the process of trying to figure out who we are as we maneuver through life, trying to survive and succeed. But basically the underlying current of this physical existence is bliss. So seeking bliss is not wrong in terms of its foundational truth. This foundation is the happiness that it experiences as pleasure. When it experiences pleasure, there is a sense of fulfillment. It is looking for something, but through outer things that are temporary, reoccurring, and only a partial piece of the bliss that exists when we begin to experience existence from the point of view of truth.

Finding one's way out of this quagmire of partial truths takes time. But if there is some clear understanding of where you are heading, some capacity to catch the structure of the old habit, to watch yourself being pulled into your outer personality, then you can start to emerge from this partial truth into a more complete truth. The more you know yourself as eternal, the more the concerns that drive the ego and the separate personality quiet, because one knows it can never die. However, the ego thinks it will die. Its foundation is identification with the personality and the body. What we are animates life; it is that which lives, that which truly is. When we live in the truth of who we are, this ability to distinguish ego from being becomes a means to come to peace, to relaxation, quietude, silence, and bliss.

FINDING ONE'S UNIQUE DHARMA

78. *Looking from the perspective of dharma you should not get perturbed either, since, for a warrior like you there is no greater cause than to fight for dharma.*
79. *Arjuna, fortunate is the warrior who gets such an opportunity to fight for a right cause. It opens the gates to heaven.*

Krishna introduces the principle of dharma. Dharma is those actions that sustain us in our purpose and our possibility. Each of us is born with this inherent possibility. All of us come into this world with the possibility of bringing forward something into creation. Our innate nature and our life and circumstances are all the opportunity for doing so. Dharma is action that is aligned with our innate nature and with the Original Intent of existence, the evolutionary movement of consciousness into Becoming. We all have a role to play in that movement, consciously or unconsciously. We are born into that as a possibility but never as a guarantee, because we have self-awareness, will, and choice. A deer or a plant doesn't have choice; we do. Dharma is a powerful concept throughout the Gita.

The Gita is saying that if we live our dharma, we are pro-gressing spiritually, whether we know it or not. Each time we succeed in manifesting our innate possibility, we move further into relationship with the truth of what we are and its inter-face with this world of creation. This fundamental principle of dharma is touched upon here and elsewhere in the Gita. We each have a unique path, a unique dharma; and finding that in ourselves, or not, determines our ability to know ourselves as this fundamental principle called the soul.

Many young people I work with suffer because they have not been able to manifest the inherent possibility they carry within them. For some people this inherent possibility is very practical, very functional; but for some it is to strive always for the highest possibility. Some of us were born to come to God, to progress on the spiritual path and develop the possi-bility of moving into the truth of who we are. Others are in an intermediary place. We each have a unique dharma. If we try to leapfrog the possibility that we carry with us, given our birth, our parents, our karma, and our conditioning, then we often have to go back and process that incomplete portion of our dharma. It acts as debris; it acts as error that weighs down our ability to progress spiritually.

Some of these errors are not in our control. Some errors are due to the randomness of circumstances. I like to say, "Life is a crapshoot." It is like the parachuters in World War II who jumped out of airplanes—some were crippled or wounded or shot. The ability to live aligned with our dharma, or not, often determines if we experience dejection or not; or it determines the poignancy or intensity of the dejection, because dejection comes also when we are not fulfilling our dharma.

How can you know? If you are living a life aligned with your inner nature, there is more happiness, more clarity, more presence, more truth. There is a sense of purpose. You have a willingness to step into life each day to do what needs to be done. There isn't fatigue or fear or depression, which comes when you have been diverted from your path of dharma. This confusion and lack of clarity and energy is due to a buildup of errors and choices not aligned with your dharma. These act as debris, making it even harder for us to move on the path.

80. *Therefore, if you refuse to fight this righteous war you will lose your fame and also incur sin from shirking your ordained duty.*
81. *People will also perpetually blame you; for a man of honor this defamation will be worse than death.*

The Gita is introducing the nature of dharma here. We will come back to it. Here, Krishna is telling Arjuna that he is already on a track and already doing what he should do. Withdrawing from his dharma will cause him great pain, and he will be forced to do it anyway because of his innate nature. Arjuna cannot withdraw from his dharma without creating sin. His true sin would be not to kill his relatives, not to destroy his attachment. Withdrawal from dharma is the true sin, not the sin that you have been trained to believe and that you imagine is true.

84. *Arjuna, if you die you will attain heaven, and if you win you will be the ruler of this earth; therefore, get up and fight with determination.*
85. *If you accept happiness and sorrow, profit and loss, victory and defeat in equal spirit and fight the battle you will never incur sin.*

Arjuna has a dilemma. His choice now is critical. He may go into error by not manifesting his innate potential—in his case, as a warrior who fights for a noble purpose or not. Krishna is revealing that when we follow the higher possibility that we all contain within, then we attain heaven even while enjoying the fruits of this earth. We attain both worlds. We gain the blessings and the bounty and the abundance of this life, as well as the blessings and the bounty of the eternal domains. We move into relationship with our true nature, allowing for peace, equanimity, and happiness.

When Arjuna surrendered to Krishna, he recognized that what he thought he knew, he in fact didn't—the third stage of ignorance. Arjuna met that part in himself that doesn't know, which is humbling. It is letting go of what you thought you knew, and is always accompanied by confusion and doubt. Trepidation arises in the moment of the beginning of any new insight that contains the possibility of moving into a truer state of knowing. Now Arjuna is hearing Krishna from a different standpoint. Arjuna recognizes that what is before him is a higher truth than he has known. He realizes the limitations of his previous truth. This is the basis of discrimination. The entire Gita is about Arjuna fulfilling his dharma. This first surrender—this first humiliation—is the beginning of many. It will take eighteen chapters for Arjuna to come to the full discrimination. It takes time for all of us. It's a process.

The Yoga of Intellect

86. *Arjuna, the wisdom that you just received belongs to the tradition of Samkhya; now hear from Me the essence of the yoga of intellect which will enable you to be free from the bondage of action.*

87. *In this approach there is no loss, no fear of contrary result nor is there any apprehension of incurring sin. Even a little progress saves one from great fear.*

88. *The intellect is focused on one goal in this approach, whereas it wanders in different directions in other approaches due to endless desires.*

The uniqueness of the Bhagavad Gita is that it points to a goal that can be intellectually grasped—the idea that you are the soul. Knowing the soul, being in relationship to the soul, and living life from that place, is one's purpose. This chapter points to the states of consciousness possible as one lives life from that place. So yoga of the intellect means that there is a trajectory, a place you are heading, in which all the actions that are arising right now are either going to take you toward or away from that goal.

The Gita points to the capacity our intellect has to discriminate, to choose differently than what we have been habituated to. It allows us to create an intent that can take us beyond what we know—a purposeful alignment of our will with a greater Will, our truth with a greater Truth. The yoga of discrimination says there is a way to live, there are actions we can take each day that can get us there. This discrimination allows us to recontextualize what arises in ourselves and in our lives as opportunities to go beyond what we have known before.

The yoga of discrimination is different from many other spiritual paths that tend to seek experience or to abide by the rules of tradition. In the Hindu tradition this is to become a renunciate, a sannyasi, to wear the ochre robes and withdraw from the world. That is what Arjuna was considering: to leave the battlefield and go into the forest. But that is only a partial truth. The Gita is pointing to a state of consciousness that goes further, one which includes life, yet is not bound by it. The yoga of discrimination does not look to just transcend this limited domain nor to seek heaven or happiness in the spiritual realms; the goal is greater than that.

In this path of discrimination, when you have set an intention to reach the goal, everything, including your faults and your errors, becomes a means of reaching it. Therefore, there is no error, no possibility of loss, because everything is converted into wisdom, into clear seeing. Every blessing is seen as a curse, and every curse is seen as a blessing. Everything becomes a means of taking you on your path. So even a fall is progress, even an error has a role to play.

This is the reassurance. The bottom line is that it is speaking to the innate authority we have—innate in our intelligence—to set a purpose, an intention, for our life. Intention has a great power, much greater than we know, because we don't know fully who we are. When that intention is aligned with the evolutionary intention, the Original Intent that came from Creation, then it is a powerfully transformative track that takes you relatively quickly to the goal. The journey is long and challenging. The secret of the Gita is to "endure calmly." Know that these feelings of happiness and sorrow are transitory and passing in nature. They do not have a basis in truth. This develops the patience and willingness needed.

89. *Unwise people cannot see beyond their literal interpretations of the Vedas and cling to their own narrow views, declaring through flowery speeches that there is nothing higher than this.*

90. *These desire-ridden seekers of heaven further proclaim that through these rites one can enjoy the fruits of action and also all riches in this life.*

Krishna is speaking to the fact that even in his time there were many, many different paths and teachings that were not in alignment with the Gita. Indian tradition has many practices and rituals in which people could move into contact with the subtle plane and have spiritual experiences. These practices and mantras became a way in which many people got stuck in new ways, because all they were doing was repeating the small experiences that were available to them through these rituals and mantras to create a new ego. They weren't progressing; they were stuck without knowing it. The ego took credit for their spiritual experiences to enhance itself. It became arrogant and confident that it could teach others, and progress stopped.

91. *Those whose minds are carried away by these narrow interpretations and who are deeply attached to pleasure and power on this earthly plane cannot obtain the determinate intellect nor also the samadhi state.*

Krishna warns of the possibility of getting diverted into paths that foster the ego's fulfillment—the senses of power, pleasure, control, and satisfaction. They were partial truths, not the full truth. They may say, "Now I am a spiritual teacher; now I have these experiences." Krishna warns of the error of those who enter the spiritual path and get a little awakening or start having experiences, then decide they have attained the final state. They create a spiritual ego and take up residence there; unwittingly attached to the temporary shallow experiences, fleeting bliss, and confidence that comes from a little attainment.

Ego clings to what it has, it doesn't want to change. Yet without the willingness to change, you cannot obtain the determinate intellect. This is a determination to reach the highest truth no matter what, to reach for something higher, to go further, to not stop when it becomes difficult, to keep going, to not rest in the little attainments, the little powers that come along the path. Only this determination will allow you to traverse the path steadily.

92. *The Vedas deal with the threefold attributes of prakriti, but one who wants liberation must go beyond these three gunas. Therefore, Arjuna, become free from the triple gunas and be established in the Self.*

This refers to the *gunas* that are detailed in Chapter 14, but a brief description will be useful here. The gunas are moods, the coloring or veils that distort our ability to know and experience reality as it is. They shape the character of our personality and influence how we see the world. The gunas are operating within us and about us all the time, constantly interacting with each other. (See Appendix III for a more in-depth description of the gunas.)

There are three guna cycles: *sattwa*, *rajas*, and *tamas*. Sattwa is the most subtle, the one closest to the origin, associated with the feeling of happiness and knowingness. Rajas is a different frequency, one of passion. It is restless and driven to action. In tamas consciousness becomes veiled and inclined to inertia and sleep. These gunas are active in everyone's system at any given time. They can be found, observed and tracked in one's system the more one progresses on the spiritual path.

Relinquishing the Fruits of Action

94. *Accept work as a matter of your right but not the fruits that come out of such works. Let not fruit be the motive of your action, and also do not be attached to inaction.*
95. *Perform all your actions as a yogi, abandoning all attachment and accepting success and failure with equal spirit. This is called yoga.*
96. *When action is performed without the yoga of intellect, it becomes inferior. Those who perform action only with a result motive deserve compassion; therefore, take refuge in the yoga of intellect while performing action.*

In these verses the Gita is beginning to address the right relationship with action, a conversation that is carried throughout its entirety. Understanding the right orientation to action is key. And the right orientation is to take action while being detached from the fruit of those actions. Take the actions required in each moment and let go of any investment in the result being other than what it is or what you want. This capacity for detached action is what the Gita is introducing in this chapter and will expand on in detail in Chapters 3 and 4.

To learn the art of getting things done without attachment, just look at your life. When you can act free from expectations and preferences for certain outcomes, there is much more energy for the action. You just do it. No big deal. But when your mind hooks in with beliefs and stories and repulsions and preferences and feelings about how you don't want to do a difficult thing, you are stuck. When you are free of those influences, the acts come spontaneously. It is joyful and satisfying. But when you are stuck, you are miserable.

In my life I had many activities that I loved. When I was younger it was making art. I loved to draw. It was enough for me just to draw. I didn't need anything else. The act was its own reward. When I was older and became involved in social work, the same thing showed up for me. There was a love of being of service to people, of helping and doing things. And later as an architect, it was the joy of doing architecture. All these actions brought their own satisfaction, including the 80 percent drudgery. I would just do what was needed without resistance. I didn't try to fight it or get out of it. I just did it. That allowed me to get things done efficiently, effectively, with the least amount of effort.

Sometimes situations arise where conditions are very difficult, and to get a little thing done you've got to work two or three times harder than you normally would. But that is what you do. You accept it. Lots of things may go wrong, but you keep taking the actions required. This lack of identification, not getting hooked in, not making a story about the difficulties and challenges and problems is the key. What is the state of consciousness that allows us to be that way? What is the state of consciousness we need to be in so that when obstacles do show up, and these frustrations and difficulties do occur, that state allows us to be in relationship with them without attachment? This is what the Gita will explain further.

THE STATE OF STABLE INTELLIGENCE

99. *When your intellect will be free from the mire of delusion you will be indifferent to what you hear and to what is yet to be heard.*

100. *When through samadhi your bewildered intellect is free from all contradictory statements and rests in the Self in a steady and undistracted position, you will attain to yoga.*

The Gita is pointing to a state of attainment that in this verse is called samadhi. Another Sanskrit word for it is *stitha prajna,* which means stable intelligence. It is when the consciousness has turned its attention away from the outer world and is dwelling on itself in a stable way. It takes much time to come to this state of stability. When we initially turn our consciousness inwardly and we get just a glimpse, it feels wonderful—and then it goes away. Then we get another glimpse and it goes away.

Why does it go away? Because of the accumulated error we all inherited—the demands, expectations, attractions, and distractions of the outer world. It is so attractive, so demanding, so full of drama, seductions, and influences that we lose our hold on these new states. The outer world keeps us endlessly distracted. The Gita points to a state of consciousness here that is turned firmly inward on the soul. It is pointing to the question, "How can I live, how can I move in this world of action and change and problems and issues?"

Arjuna said:

101. *Krishna, what are the signs of a person who has attained the samadhi state? How does he speak, live and interact with others?*

The Blessed Lord said:

102. *Arjuna, when a person is able to free himself completely from the desires of the mind and is able to enjoy the bliss of the Self, then he is said to have attained the samadhi state.*
103. *When a person is not perturbed in a situation of sorrow, is not attracted to pleasure, and is free from attachment, fear, and anger, he is said to have attained the samadhi state.*
104. *When one is free from infatuation and adoration and neither rejoices at achievement nor feels dejected by adversity, he is said to have attained the state of equanimity.*
105. *Like a tortoise withdrawing his limbs from all directions, a man who has attained equanimity is capable of withdrawing his senses from objects of pleasure at will.*

These verses describe the symptoms of one who has attained this "stable intelligence," the samadhi state. They describe what it would look like and feel like to be completely free from the desires of the mind and to enjoy the bliss of the self. *"When a person is not perturbed in a situation of sorrow, is not attracted to pleasure, and is free from attachment, fear, and anger"* or *"when one is free from infatuation and adoration, and neither rejoices at achievement nor feels dejected by adversity, he is said to have attained the state of equanimity."*

Equanimity is another description of the stitha prajna state, the samadhi state. It is the ability to have all things be equal. Pain and pleasure are equal. Happiness and sadness are equal. One is not better than the other. Moving into relationship with the dualities of this existence by allowing for both without a preference is the state of equanimity.

It is also reflected within yourself. In the state of equanimity you are in a state of inner stillness and quietude. Even when perturbations rise up, something you could get excited about or upset by—they are all equal. They are just energies. They are just things that are happening. You are resting in the still center of existence. You are the still presence in which existence arises. It is a state of consciousness free from the endless ping-pong of life, feeling good, feeling bad, this or that. It is beyond the matrix of entanglement, of bondage, of veiling.

CLOSING THE REACTIVITY GAP

106. *When a seeker abstains from pleasures for a long time, his senses turn away from the objects; however, the taste for them persists in him. This relish also disappears when a person experiences the Supreme in samadhi state.*
107. *Arjuna, so turbulent are the senses that even the mind of a wise man who has practiced self-control is carried away forcibly by them.*
108. *To be linked with Me and to retain that state one must control his senses. When the senses are under control one attains the state of equanimity.*

Here is the secret—This is the key: Learn to control the senses, to control the signals that come in from the outside world through our sight, smell, sound, touch, taste. These signals are what keep us constantly dancing in our egoic habit, in our identity as an ego. When a signal comes in—something someone said, maybe some gossip or a piece of news—it activates a mechanism within ourselves for good or ill. So controlling the senses really means controlling the sources of our reaction to the bombardment of the senses.

The senses are a means to experience outer life. Therefore, when we begin to control the senses, we begin to control our outer life by withdrawing our consent to act out our impulses and reactions. We do this by taking a pause, stepping in at the moment of the arising of the signal, and choosing not to act. This capacity to control the senses takes time, because without us knowing it, by our unwitting complete identification to our body—vital and mind—we are run by impulsiveness and the mechanism of reacting and responding to signals. By restraining those signals, by training ourselves over time to become present and to notice how a signal affects us—to catch it just before it causes us to act, either with anticipation, enthusiasm, desire, or repulsion, fear or anger—we can choose to act or not act. We can withdraw our consent to be overtaken by the signals that come from the senses. But it takes time.

Let's say that an event happens. Somebody says something. We get angry and blow up at them. We make them wrong. We create sorrow and disturbance for both people. We both go off to our own rooms and are sitting there dwelling on it, trying to make ourselves right, trying to find a way to resolve it, either blaming the other person or blaming ourselves. Maybe after enough time passes we reflect, "Wow, look at what happened. Look at what overtook me. I could have done something differently." So a gap occurs between the event of the sensory input and our waking up to the fact that we were in reaction. Previously we are the reaction. We don't know we are in reaction—we "are" the reaction. "They are an asshole. They just betrayed us. They said the wrong thing. They insulted us." We are triggered. We are the reaction. We are just a conditioned egoic identification. We are then not the soul but the vehicle. We are the *jiva* bound in the world of samskara, of impressions.

In that consciousness we don't know jack shit. We are just being bounced around this way and that. The distance between that occurring and becoming aware is a measure of our state of equanimity. The more often you catch yourself reacting, the shorter length of time it takes to come to choice. Instead of two or three days later, maybe it's the next day. Instead of twelve hours later, it becomes eight hours, four hours, two hours. The more we move into presence with that unconscious mechanism that is running us, the more we can begin to control the reaction.

When you actually come to present time with what is arising, you will notice you have a choice. You still have a choice to run one way or another, toward enthusiasm and anticipation or toward fear, anger, and judgment. In the moment of choice you've come to the possibility of equanimity. Presence and equanimity are the same thing. Presence and samadhi are the same thing. The ability to be here now with what is arising is the same thing. The more we restrain our impulses—the more we restrain our reactions, the more determinate our intelligence becomes—the more the soul is able to come forth and express itself through discrimination between what is true and what is not true; and the more we move into the samadhi state. The key is restraining the senses.

Now this might be as small as controlling the impulse for eating. It could be as small as controlling the impulse to play on the computer, to go onto the dating site to seek new relationships. Or it might be as small as simply restraining these little minor activities and redesigning them so that they fit according to your intent.

Restraining the inclination of the senses is the most powerful tool in reshaping the identification of your consciousness with itself as the "who"—the persona, the person, the *jiva*, the personality, the ego—to the "what," the truth of you as the soul, the Self, the being.

SPIRITUAL FALL

109. *Attachment to the senses comes when the consciousness is allowed to dwell on sense objects. From attachment comes desire and from desire comes anger.*

110. *From anger comes delusion and from delusion comes confusion of memory. Due to a confused memory, reasoning is clouded and one loses the capacity to discriminate. When this capacity is lost one is completely ruined.*

This is Gita's warning. If you let the signals from the world overtake you, there is the danger of a spiritual fall. This happens because you are not aware you have been overtaken. The signal comes suddenly through the senses (something said, heard, or seen), and you become the reaction, the desire, or the fear that arises. You have been activated, either through repulsion or attraction, to a person or situation. You become attached to a certain outcome, for things to go a certain way. If you act on this impulse you become further entangled, and the thoughts, feelings, or sensations become more compelling. You have become identified, attached to the outcome. You have become invested. An attraction, a want, a fear, or a repulsion has been activated. Once this happens, your consciousness has become obscured by these things. The quality of your soul's radiance becomes absorbed in what is arising.

Once this happens you become an instrument, a tool of what has been activated. The whole system goes into agreement. The mind rationalizes and justifies, creating a story that feeds what has overtaken you. "They didn't act the way I wanted. They didn't give me the feedback I wanted to hear. They are not showing appreciation for me." From here we fall further. Anger arises.

And then comes confusion of memory. We distort the facts to support our righteous position. We argue. It doesn't make any difference what happened, it is whatever I imagined or would choose to remember about what happened. And with the confusion of memory, reason is clouded. You have lost track of what really happened. You are caught up in the ego and its machinery.

And of course at that point you lose all capacity to discriminate. And when you have lost that, you are completely ruined. You have been sucked in. Down the rabbit hole. In the black pit. Gone. This happens again and again. How many times a day this happens is usually a measure of where you are in relationship with the truth of yourself—where you are in equanimity.

THE SAMADHI STATE

111. *But one who is established in samadhi and has obtained the capacity of being neutral to likes and dislikes can derive the benefits from objects of pleasure at will while maintaining serenity.*
112. *With serenity comes the end of all sorrow, and the intellect of such a seeker remains easily fixed on the Self . . .*
113. *Therefore, Arjuna, know it for certain that the person whose senses are completely restrained is the one who has attained the state of equanimity.*

Samadhi is a state of absorption with the source of consciousness, the Absolute, the Sat. Equanimity is a state of consciousness that comes with exposure to this samadhi state. This process in time dissolves all that separates us from this absolute condition of consciousness. Fear, lack, want, need, desire all dissolve in this state. What remains is a condition of immediacy and presence in which all that arises is a manifestation of this all-pervading reality. Nothing is missing or needed. Past and future lose their relevancy. All there is, is the timeless Now.

117. *As the sea is ever unchanged although it receives all the waters, so also a man of equanimity is always at peace even though all desires enter into him.*
118. *The man who has given up all desire and is free from longing, egoism, and hankering is fit to attain supreme peace.*
119. *Arjuna, this is known as the supreme divine state. When such a state is attained one is no longer deluded even at the time of leaving the body, and remaining in the state he reaches the state of nirvana.*

But for the samadhi state to establish itself, one must control the pull of their senses to the outer world. This helps turn the consciousness inward toward its source, thus strengthening the samadhi state. The two together effect a fundamental shift in consciousness that brings the symptoms these verses describe.

In this state, everything is accepted, everything is allowed, everything has permission to exist, yet you rest unperturbed in this state of truth. *"As the sea is ever unchanged although it receives all the waters"*—negative, positive, poison, bliss, all the waters—*"so also a man of equanimity is always at peace even though all desires,"*—experiences, all inclinations, all impulses—*"enter into him."* It is all experienced, all felt, yet we are always absorbed in the poise of the truth of what we are. This is the ultimate discrimination. This is the message of the second chapter. What is the state, the attitude, the orientation of consciousness that we can bring into life that brings forward this highest possibility? This we'll explore in more depth in the next chapter, The Yoga of Action.

CHAPTER 3

The Yoga of Action

But the man who always dwells in the Self, derives satisfaction
from the Self and is able to enjoy the delight of the Self,
for him there is no karma.
࿇ **VERSE 136**

The Bhagavad Gita is something that you live. The goal is not
to live in some abstract, faraway zone of bliss, or only to
experience revelation. The most powerful tool of the individual
self-aware human being is the yoga of action. It is the most
powerful tool, because it reveals how to live in collaboration
with the matter and spirit of each of us. It brings together that
part which is human and that part which is divine.

THE IMPERATIVE FOR ACTION

Action is key throughout the Gita. Some actions we can't
avoid. This is what Arjuna is facing. He is trying to get out of
the battle. Krishna is reminding Arjuna that going off into the
woods isn't going to do it. If everybody goes off and transcends
into nirvana, the world will be left in chaos. There is a reason
we were born into these bodies. This Earth is the home, the
Mother, in which consciousness can wake up to itself. If we

transcend this domain of bodies, minds, and emotions, we go to the Father; we go to the origin, to the Sat. But then we leave the Mother behind.

To not return back down and assist the Mother in her evolutionary purpose is shirking the job. That is why action is such an important conversation throughout the entire Gita. Our purpose is not just to free ourselves from our habituated, programmed, egoic existence so that we can return to our original transcendent, pure condition. It is also to bring that pure condition into life, bring it back to the Mother, bring it back to the seat of "what" we are, integrate it and make it real. In that way we lift the collective consciousness.

THE GITA AS AN INTEGRAL PATH

The Gita is an integral spiritual path. It includes all aspects of our nature: mental, emotional, and physical. In order for the Gita to be integral, it has to have a different yoga, a path, for each aspect of our nature. These are the path of knowledge, the path of love or devotion, and the path of action. They are interwoven in each chapter. Yet of the three, the Gita gives the most emphasis to the path of action. It says that no matter what your understanding, insight, revelation, or spiritual experience is, or what sense of awe or connection you have, without action your experiences cannot be integrated. They cannot be brought together. They cannot be lived, developed, and made part of your reality, part of your day-to-day life. This is the purpose, to make them real.

We become oriented to any of these three paths based on our innate nature. If your mental aspect is very developed, then the path of knowledge or awareness comes naturally to you, and you tend to grow more rapidly along that path. If you are inclined more toward feelings or emotions, then the path of devotion comes more naturally to you, and you tend to be drawn to that. If your system is more physical, more *rajasic*, then the path you are inclined to is action.

The Power of Action

The capacity for conscious action is the power that has been given to self-aware humans. When awareness became aware of itself, it stepped out of the morass of impulse and reaction, of instinct and conditioning. It stepped out of the programming of nature and stepped into a possibility of choosing. We are speaking here of conscious action—not impulsive, instinctual, or reactive actions, which come from our human nature programming, from the evolution of the body, and from the psychological conditioning of childhood.

When we choose something for good or for ill, for high or for low, it impacts others and the world in ways that are much greater than we can know. With action we can change our nature, we can change others and the world. We can create, discover, and invent. We break out of the box that nature created. The human being's ability to impact the world is greater than any other living creature. The power of that effectiveness comes from the intelligence and will of self-awareness. This self-will, this ability to choose to act, is unique to the self-aware human being.

Understanding the power of action is perhaps the most useful technology of the Bhagavad Gita—understanding, first, that every time we choose to take an action or to restrain an impulse to act, we bring something new into existence. So if you apply your will and choose one morning to exercise when your inclination is not to exercise, then you become more powerful by breaking out of the inertia of your ordinary life. You create a new possibility for being on that day. This application of will is an effort, a sacrifice of something old for something new. Therefore, choosing to do something like exercise means you are breaking out of the inclination and creating a new way to be in that part of your life.

This is the power of action. The more we choose, through intelligent will, actions that are aligned with the higher good, with truth and oneness, the more we make those real. The more we take actions that are aligned with ego, untruth, separateness, fear, need, or lack, the more we reinforce those things. So our actions are evidence of what we are empowering: the ego or the truth of our being. It is your choice even when you choose someone to guide you. You choose to accept their guidance. This, too, is a powerful action.

The Matrix of Interconnectivity

Action has ramifications throughout all creation. Why? Because we are all in a matrix of interconnection. Any being who takes an action creates a vibration throughout the entire matrix, the entire web. This web of interconnectedness is a field of consciousness into which we are all born and live. A spider that sits on its web feels when a fly comes in. The spider knows this through vibration. When we take an action we are affecting everyone and everything all around us. This is especially so with those that you are most connected with, the parts of the web that are most intimate or personal to you. It doesn't have to be just a physical matrix; it is a matrix of consciousness. Everything is interconnected.

Actions cause ripples, or consequences. Consequences are for good, for ill, or neutral. Every time we take or don't take an action, it has an effect on the existing matrix in which we are living. Of course it is endlessly changing because there are innumerable beings on the planet, including seven billion people. The choices we make can have the power to affect the matrix. These come through us, through our intelligent will, our aspiration, the drive to bring forward something that doesn't currently exist.

Action that Binds, Action that Liberates

Action is key throughout the Gita—conscious, yogic, purposeful action. Other forms of action are not purposeful. They are driven by impulse, inclination, attraction, or repulsion. They are driven by preferences and desires, wants and frustrations. These actions perpetuate bondage; they keep us entangled— like a ball of string—a bundle of karma that we are continuously winding and unwinding. As long as we are being driven by these inclinations, we are just perpetuating the existing condition and assuring future bondage. We are also perpetuating everybody else's bondage, wrapping more string in their ball of stories and beliefs, habits and ideas. It's a continuous process, this wrapping and accumulating of karma and consequences, avoiding experiences, staying in unconscious habitual existence.

Action done impulsively without thinking binds you. And it perpetuates itself because it carries the power that expresses itself through you in creation. As long as you are operating unconsciously, you are an unwitting instrument for the error of the evolutionary process. This is karma; this is more delusion. You can only break this cycle through yogic action, purposeful action based on our interconnectedness, on oneness and truth—the Brahman, the Sat. This is action aligned with the purpose of existence, the Original Intent, that first primal urge to exist and to come into a fully expressed manifest condition.

The dharma of Nature is to manifest. That is the work of existence. It is happening everywhere, unconsciously, through action. And in the process a lot of errors are made. A lot of consequences are created along the way. And as long as these errors exist, the capacity of Nature to evolve is very slow, rising and falling over thousands and thousands of years.

But when we wake up and become aware of ourselves, we begin to understand that we are not just a human being, that we have a soul, and we can discover the capacity to discriminate between what is true and what is not true. We are not this bound, locked-up structure of habits, this wound-up Energizer Bunny acting out its reactions and unconscious impulses. We are something other than that. We are the animating principle.

We are the foundational structure in which these things actually run. We are the juice, the power. When we wake up to that, yogic action is possible. Purposeful action is possible. Prior to that it is not.

This drive is consciousness itself. It is the motivating principle of all creation. It arises from the Original Intent. When we take an action, knowingly or not, we have an intent. The intent is to have more pleasure, or to be liked at work, or to get along with people, or to protect ourselves, or to get what we think we want. We use intention, the power of self-aware consciousness, to bring something into existence. As soon as we act on that intention, it begins to manifest. An action can be something that you say, something you communicate through your computer, or a movement—all the different modalities of actions. Even thought is an action. Action based on our choices can keep things the same or create a new way of being in the world. In the same way choosing not to act can change things or keep things as they are. This world we live in and how it shows up for us is the consequence of all actions ever taken or not taken, consciously or unconsciously, by Nature or man.

To change the way we are currently relating to existence, just look at your actions. Look at what you put attention to. Look at what you do. Look at the food you eat, the conversations you have, your judgments, what you do when someone calls you on your reactions, especially the ones you get swept away with. All of these can let you know you are in a paradigm, an existing point of view, a relationship with this entire matrix.

Of course this ability to act consciously is also true in the material life. If we want to do well at school, then we study. We apply effort, because our inclination is not to study hard but to watch TV, relax, hang out with our friends, play football, or whatever. We study hard because we were taught that would help us reach a higher goal. We act in alignment with that purpose. And the more we study, the better we get at studying.

It's the same principle on the spiritual path. The more you put your attention on the spiritual path, the more strength and determination is available to you. The more your acts are aligned, the more real the spiritual path becomes for you. It's that simple. We carry within us the power to create realities other than the ones to which we have become habituated. If we have an insight or a realization and don't act to bring it into our lives, then it is just philosophy, just theory, something you can write a book about. It has very little power to change your reality or to change the reality of other people, other than perhaps on the mental plane. If you have a spiritual experience and you are suddenly thrown into a relationship to something greater than yourself but you don't start aligning your life with what that spiritual experience is pointing to, if you don't prepare yourself to be more receptive to those experiences, then it fades away, becoming just a memory.

KNOWLEDGE VERSUS ACTION

In the second chapter, the Yoga of Discrimination, Krishna pointed to the signs of what happens as one brings the eternal, unchanging quality of our true nature into one's life. This ability to consciously be in touch with the soul is knowledge. The ability to be free from attachment, to stand back and witness oneself, is to know the samadhi state. But in the very first part of Chapter 3, to which we turn now, Arjuna asks, "Why are you teaching me this? What is the use of it? How is this relevant? Why is this knowledge important if you are at the same time wanting me to take action in the world?"

Let's begin with Chapter 3, The Yoga of Action (Karma Yoga).

Arjuna said:

120. *Krishna, if you know that knowledge is superior to action, then why do you urge me to perform this terrible action?*

121. *Your words are conflicting and confuse my intellect, therefore, please recommend a path for me that will definitely take me to the highest goal.*

Arjuna can't grasp the point of the second chapter yet. It is still too new for him. Discrimination is still just an idea. Knowing the soul is just an idea. Equanimity, samadhi, and nirvana are just abstractions. How are they relevant to the fact that he is standing on a battlefield and sixteen million people are ready to kill each other? He is impatient, but at the same time knows that he doesn't know. He has humility. He is saying, "Your words are conflicting and confusing, therefore please recommend a path that will definitely take me to the highest good."

This is a point that will be repeated again and again. There is no teaching unless there is listening, unless there is a capacity to learn. Without receptivity there will be no transmission. Without Arjuna's humility the Gita could not have been revealed. Without listening there is no Gita. And if you are just listening with the mental, then you only get whatever you can through the mind. If the other parts of you are closed—you don't get it. Listening is actually through your whole body. The body listens, the vital listens, the mind listens.

Humility and receptivity allow learning. This is early in the journey, so it is still primarily in Arjuna's mind, or your mind. Each of us is different. Arjuna was a mental being. His innate inclination was to know and to act, but you will see him change as he goes through each stage of the journey.

The Blessed Lord said:

122. *Arjuna, to reach the highest state I have shown two approaches to people in this world long ago. One is through the technique of knowledge for the followers of Samkhya*

and the other is through the technique of yogic action for the followers of yoga.

123. *Simply by withdrawing from outer activity one cannot reach the state of actionlessness; so also the state of perfection cannot be attained by mere renunciation of outer action.*

124. *No one can ever remain inactive, even for a moment, because all are helplessly driven to action by their innate qualities born of nature.*

Krishna is beginning to reveal two essential paths, the path of knowledge and the path of action. There is a third, the path of devotion, which will be revealed later. The path of knowledge is the traditional spiritual path: to be in the revelatory state, to expand your awareness, to transcend. This tradition of transcending is reflected in the ancient Indian philosophy of *samkhya*, which basically says to leave the world. When you renounce the world—your attachments, your ideas, your habits and beliefs—the truth of what you are comes more and more to the surface.

This knowledge takes you into relationship with your soul. This is also the spiritual path prevalent in our culture. It is to transcend, to stay transcended, to stay in the witness, to come to the no-self, to abide in the nondual state—as in the Buddhist and the Advaitic traditions. This is the prevalent teaching, currently and also at the time of the Gita.

But Krishna is saying that knowledge alone, transcendence alone, won't do it. You will not be able to stay in that state of knowing if you stay isolated from the world. You must engage in life. It is only when you engage in action that you can strengthen your capacity to be present with what is arising. This ability to be present, to be conscious and not sucked into your reactions, beliefs, opinions, and ideas of what you should be doing, gives you the ability to choose to act or not to act. It is a place of intelligent poise. It is a place of coming to the present moment as it is. As your reactions come to you, either through your senses or inwardly, you then are able to witness them with sufficient detachment—a witnessing capacity in which you don't get overtaken, you don't lose yourself. This state of being able to choose, this poise, is called actionlessness. It is not something we do, rather it is the result of having reached a state of consciousness called samadhi. Samadhi is a state of absorption with the soul. It gives one the ability to be present with what is arising without getting sucked into it.

"All are helplessly driven to action by their innate qualities born of nature." We have been programmed from birth. We have been conditioned by our body, by our culture, and by the inclinations and trainings that our parents received from their parents and our grandparents received from their parents. We have been born into a conditioned environment where what we are as consciousness has gotten tangled up into a specific structure, a web matrix in which the world appears a certain way to us. It is either a fear-based paradigm, where it is all threatening, or a desire-based paradigm, where it is all a fruit basket. It is a point of view that we inherited.

We are, of course, a mix of all of these things. Without realizing it, we are being lived by these conditioned things, rather than living life directly. These are our stories. They run us. They tell us what we like and don't like, what we can do and can't do. Our ideas of what is possible are defined by this matrix that we inherited, qualities born of nature and nurture. We are helplessly driven by them. Krishna is pointing out that we are bound and don't know it. We are caught up in a web without even knowing there is a web. This is how life is, we think. From within the web, escape is not possible. We have to find something that stands outside. And that is what the soul is.

Action that Leads to Perfect Actionlessness

125. *One who outwardly restrains the organs of action but mentally dwells on the objects of senses is verily deluded and is a hypocrite.*

The Gita is saying that those who outwardly believe the scriptures and practice the mantras or rituals but have not brought it into their lives are deluded. It is not integrated and therefore not real. That lack of integration is hypocrisy. You say something, but you do something else. You believe you are one way, but you are actually another way. One part of you is awake but hasn't been integrated, hasn't been made real.

126. *Controlling the senses through the mind and remaining unattached, if one can perform action as means to yoga through the instruments only, he can attain perfection.*

Integration is accomplished through acts of sacrifice, such as the effort of controlling the senses through the mind and remaining unattached. Restraining the senses is restraining the inclination that comes with your nature—the way you are programmed to think, feel, and want. Through such restraint you begin to recover your ability to choose. Recovering your authority in that particular area of your life will, in time, take you to perfection. But even here you have to be detached from the outcome. You have to be willing to go through the process of changing your relationship with existence to enter a new way of being. This shift is quite difficult. Without detachment it is impossible, because you will constantly be pulled to go back to the familiar.

So the Gita says, *"If one can perform action as a means to yoga through the instrument only, he can attain perfection."*

In other words, Krishna is saying that if you can actually live life, if you can be in life acting as required in the moment, yet detached from the outcome of those actions, then life is your spiritual practice. It is the Yoga of Action. You bring your awareness of the truth of what you are into life by doing whatever is necessary. Being detached—not attached to any particular benefit or profit from it—will bring you to this state of action-lessness. The more you are engaged in this kind of action, the more perfect is your actionlessness.

127. *Perform the works that are ordained for you because action is better than inaction. Moreover, even your body cannot be sustained without action.*

The Gita says that to perform your ordained actions is better than inaction. Action is better than inaction because we become more masterful in the process of encountering that which resists, that which opposes, that which is difficult. Ordained action is the required action, your dharma—the right action for you at this stage of your life. One's dharma may be to work—to be a mother or father and raise children, to have a job and support the family. We all have the dharma to grow and develop as an individual, to become an individual ego. A child has a dharma, a student has a dharma, an adolescent has a dharma, a young adult has a dharma, a mature adult has a dharma. One's dharma constantly shifts throughout life.

But when we come to the spiritual path, we have one dharma: to know truth, to know God. That is the *satyadharma,* the highest dharma. When we have come to the spiritual path, then our dharma is the action that supports our spiritual progress. We come out of our personal individual nature and develop our impersonal universal nature.

Sacrifice as a Means to Undo the False Self

128. *Action becomes a cause of bondage in the world only when it is not performed as a sacrifice; therefore, perform action efficiently as a sacrifice only, without being attached.*

This is a crucial point. When you change from what you are inclined to do and instead do something that is aligned with your intelligent will, there is a gap. Sacrifice is the entry point into this gap. There is what you are inclined to do, and then there is what your intelligent will says you should be doing. To bridge that gap takes effort. It is a sacrifice. This is the key.

Anytime you apply effort to do something contrary to your inclination, you strengthen your discrimination, your intelligent consciousness. You develop the capacity for determination and persistence. And every time you don't, you weaken that part of yourself; you stay bound by your innate or habitual inclinations. Action taken aligned with your higher Self creates a momentum, a force that pulls you out of your attachment to the old ways and in the process strengthens your ability to manifest your intent.

This is how we recover what we really are. Sacrifice is how we undo the false self. Sacrifice is how we break up the selfish structures of ego. Being selfish is not our fault. We were born into this orientation. When we sacrifice we are not just doing it for ourselves. We are a piece of the entire matrix. We are one seven-billionth of the problem, and we are one seven-billionth of the solution. When we shift, the whole matrix shifts. So our sacrifice is actually a service, a bringing forward of a higher possibility for everyone. To do this, to apply this effort, this discipline, is the foundational principle of the Gita.

Nothing in nature needs to sacrifice consciously. In this Creation, all things living know instinctively their role in the balance of things. They sacrifice instinctively, without conscious effort, to forage for food, to protect their young. However, man is not ruled as much by instinct and biology and has to choose to sacrifice. Though mankind loses this natural connection, it also gains the capacity to go beyond Nature. Mankind carries this capacity to manifest the Original Intent more perfectly; however, we have to sacrifice to do so. We have to go beyond the inertia and limitation of Nature and the limitation of our biological origins. But it is this conscious sacrifice that has the power to create new realities, new possibilities for Existence.

When we choose to sacrifice, when we control our mind, our moods and feelings, our senses, we evoke a power that allows us to move into alignment with the Original Intent and its evolutionary purpose. We step out of our existing condition and move into a new, less-conditioned state of being. In this sense all effort is creative, be it for ill or good. Effort can serve the ego or serve a higher purpose. If effort serves the ego, then the power of that sacrifice goes to the ego. If effort serves a higher purpose, then the power goes to the higher purpose. If the purpose is to manifest the soul, then that is what gets empowered. If the purpose is to manifest the ego, then that is what gets empowered.

When we are able to take action in a state of equanimity—without a preference, without having one thing more important than the other, simply handling whatever is coming up, be it difficult or easy, be it good or bad, be it pleasurable or painful—our sacrifice is more powerful. We act only as required in each moment—not adding, changing, or controlling. The key is to *perform action efficiently as a sacrifice only, without being attached.* These words reveal one who is in the state of equanimity, who is already in conscious samadhi. For them, all action is performed without effort, efficiently, as a sacrifice.

SACRIFICE IS A MEANS TO SURRENDER

Sacrifice can become surrender. Sacrifice is the first step. Sacrifice is required when resistance is strong, making it difficult to move into a new way of being. But if we persist, the sacrifice becomes less and less difficult. We do it without effort. Consider exercise. If you haven't exercised for a while, it is difficult to start. And the only way to continue is through regular application of effort. You begrudge the difficulty but do it anyway. After some time of doing this, not as much effort is required. You start feeling something is happening; you feel pretty good. The effort has become easier. It is satisfying not only because you are getting stronger, but because you feel good at the same time. Action has become effortless. It's no longer a sacrifice. The action becomes its own reward.

This is the idea of sacrificing without attachment to the outcome. Surrender is the principle of action for its own fulfillment, without needing a certain outcome. Some actions are satisfying in themselves. As an artist, after a point, I became absorbed in the project and it became effortless. But at first I had to apply effort to get myself into the modality of drawing. Once I got into the modality of drawing, the fruit came naturally. The action brought its own fulfillment, its own joy. It didn't need a particular result or an outcome.

CREATION IS SUSTAINED BY SACRIFICE

129. *At the time of creation the creator god created human beings through sacrifice and advised them, "By this you multiply; let this yield you the enjoyments you seek."*

When we act as a sacrifice, we are not acting; it is creation acting through us. That is what is expressed here. But what is that action? It is self-giving. It is a giving up of ourselves, like the ocean gives up its moisture into the atmosphere, the atmosphere gives up its moisture as rain, saturating the soil, and the soil gives up its moisture to the plants that grow, and the plants sacrifice themselves for the animals that graze on them. Through sacrifice the world order is maintained.

Creation is sustained by sacrifice. Even at the physical level it is sustained by sacrifice. When we consciously begin to take self-giving action, giving up of something that we are habituated to for something we do not yet know, we bring forward in that moment the power of truth consciousness—the power of intelligent will, *chit shakti*, the original force from which this entire creation emerged. We move more in touch with that which is the truth of us, the soul, the being. So the path of action is a process of self-giving, of renouncing, of letting go of preferences and comforts and ideas, of giving yourself to something greater.

132. *The virtuous do not incur sin because they accept the rewards of sacrifice after offering to the gods, but those who are selfish do not share the results of their work with the gods and therefore reap the consequence of their sinful act.*

When we take action that serves our ego, our benefit, fear, comfort, familiarities, ideas, and beliefs, then we eat the sin of those acts. We poison ourselves by reinforcing the very principle that separates us from the soul. We separate ourselves every time we indulge ourselves, every time we feed our habits, every time we believe our story, our beliefs, every time we allow a negative reaction to occur. That is when karma, which in one sense means action, becomes karma in the other sense, which means the residue, the consequence of those acts. The consequence of those acts coats us like debris. We accumulate these acts that serve the separate self, and we strengthen the veil of the separate self.

133. *All beings come from food, food comes from rain, rain comes from sacrifice, and sacrifice is rooted in action.*

Our purpose on this planet is to sacrifice for something other than our individual egoic sense of self, be it mental or emotional or physical. Without this self-giving we remain bound. If we have an expectation associated with our giving, if we are attached to the giving, then this, too, is bondage. If we give for any reason other than to give, if we give for any reason other than as an offering to lift the world in whatever way we can see by our light, then we continue to create bondage. If our expectation for reward determines whether we feel good about giving or not, if we feel resentful or not, we have set ourselves up for more suffering. As soon as we have expectations, we are back into karma. Even if they are fulfilled, it is still karma. And if they are not fulfilled, then it is also karma. It is just karma, karma, and more karma until you wake up to the truth of the "what" you are. Then your actions become yogic. You operate in a poised state of consciousness, undoing the separate self and revealing the soul.

134. *Actions originate from Brahman, the Imperishable. Therefore, the all-pervading Imperishable is always present in sacrifice.*

This last verse is a very powerful statement. When we take action aligned with the Brahman, we are taking divine action. We are taking action that arises from the Original Intent, that place from which all action arises. This is the Brahman. We are moving into alignment with that which acts, that which can act, that intelligence and will present in the seminal possibility of consciousness.

Unwinding
In the Gita, yogic action isn't about living in a cave or an ashram, or going to seminars or taking online courses, or

reading spiritual books. Rather everything arising in your life becomes an opportunity for yogic action. It is all an opportunity to bring truth, consciousness, and love into your daily actions, whatever they may be. Life is an opportunity to observe your actions from a place of manifesting yourself as the soul, as the occupying presence. From that inward alertness, what you do outwardly is secondary.

Certainly, try to have your actions be effective, to produce the results that are needed. If you are washing dishes, then wash the dishes the best that you can so that the dishes are as clean as they can be. That's the perfect expression of the truth in the moment. Somehow the dishes need to be done. Maybe it was your turn. Maybe someone yelled at you about not doing your dishes. Whatever the reason, you do the dishes from that yogic place. You just do it without expecting praise. You just do the dishes. Then no matter what role you have, be it a husband, wife, businessman, warrior, it doesn't matter, because everything in your life becomes *sadhana*—spiritual practice.

The key to yogic action is to reclaim action as a means of transcending the habitual activity of the tangle of karma, of consequences, the ocean of *samskaras* and *vasanas,* the inherited tendencies and inclinations. This is how we begin to unwind this ball of string, this tangle of our bondage. This is how we begin to unwind the existing inclinations and tendencies. When we start acting without an investment in the outcome, without wanting a certain kind of result, without expecting to be rewarded or for it to come out a certain way, we begin to unwind those inclinations in us. Each time we do, we neutralize these inclinations and begin to disengage from the habit of our dissatisfaction, our whining. There is endless whining. "I don't have what I want, I don't like it the way it is, I want it different." That's whining, right? You feed the dissatisfaction when you whine, feed the inclination to whine. Want to know if you are creating karma? Notice if you are whining.

You can only unwind something if you are aware you are doing it. You have to be resting in a different place than the normal egoic paradigm.

This different place comes when you have a sense of your soul, a sense of that quiet, still inner presence that lives you. Then yogic action is possible. Before yogic action is possible, discrimination is needed. Then you can know the difference between what binds you and what does not. Everybody is habituated to action that creates bondage. Everybody is used to swimming in this ocean of *samskara,* this delusion. How do we come out of it? By waking up and then by taking conscious, intentional action.

We start by controlling the senses. We hear that somebody has said something derogatory about us, and we become over-taken by a reaction. All these actions and reactions are karma. Impulse and reaction creates bondage and delusion. When you hear a derogatory statement and you find yourself activated, notice: "Look at this. I am activated. I am plugged in." The object of your senses is spinning you. The tail is wagging the dog. There's almost no dog. The dog is this little thing and the tail is this huge thing. The tail is wagging this little dog that hasn't gotten big enough to resist the wagging of the tail.

At first you only have enough awareness to notice that you are being wagged. You are being whipped around by habitual programming. To detach the tail, to cut the object of the senses, you have to become conscious and quit believing the story it tells you. You have to withdraw your consent to run down that track, to get revenge, or to beat yourself up and go into guilt and doubt. You have to resist the temptation to come back and retaliate or gossip or try to create agreement for your position or to defeat their position. All of that just feeds the endless web you are entangled in.

Such endless whining runs everything. It is the human atmosphere. When you step out of that atmosphere and then descend back into it, you would say, "Argh, who would want to be here?" So cut your investment. Choose to take yogic action and become present with that which is arising in you. Recognize yourself as the source of your own experience. Decide to find a way to accept or forgive whatever it is that came to you. "OK, this is what happened. They said this. I heard this. I had this reaction." And become present with that reaction and notice how it turns your gut, how your mind keeps whirling, how you can't get to sleep. You say, "OK, here are the consequences. This is what's going on." When you are with it enough, it starts to lose its ability to wag you, to grip you. You develop a capacity to notice yourself. You become capable of self-inquiry. We will get to this in Chapter 4.

LIVING WITHOUT A TRACE

136. *But the man who always dwells in the Self, derives satisfaction from the Self, and is able to enjoy the delight of the Self, for him there is no karma.*

That's a summary of what I have been saying. The Gita is using the word "Self" to mean the unconditioned state of the soul versus the conditioned state of ego or the "self": the "what" we are versus the "who" we are. When we are able to *dwell in the Self,"* through spiritual practice and meditation, we begin to rest in that state of consciousness. We step out of the usual human paradigm; we transcend the habit of our little self, our egoic doingness. When we are in that transcendent state and then come back down into the world, we don't get overtaken as much. It's easier to let go of our reactions and preferences. We have more ability to say "No" to our habitual inclinations. For one who is able to derive satisfaction from that state of consciousness, who has the ability to appreciate the value of being connected to the Self, the challenges and concerns of the outer world become less. Then one can step back and look at what arises without getting caught up in it.

This came up for me recently. I was noticing my system was rajasic. I was going through my day and I noticed a lot of things were not working. I was paying attention to the part of me that was pushing, the part that was restless to get things done. Rajas puts me into future time where I am not with what I am doing, because I am anticipating the next thing I want to do. Standing in the grocery line it came up, and I thought, "This is going to take too much time. There are four people in front of me, and the cashier is going about it in his own way—not the way my rajas wants it." I noticed this going on inside, and how awful it is to be in rajas! And I was OK. I was not changing anything. I knew I had to be patient; part of my ego was restless, but my being just waited. It wasn't pleasant or unpleasant; it was just waiting.

Without this sense of connection to the Self, you will believe that you are your mood; that you are a particular cycle of restlessness, or obscurity, or resistance. Even though the rajas was going on and it was irritating, there was no karma because I did not act on it. So there is no trace left, no residue. As soon as I leave the situation, it disappears. There is no projection of difficulty into the future. There is no need to, because when rajas is going on, it is simply rajas arising in the moment. The bottom line is that it is not adding or taking anything away from what is arising. It is just what is arising. In that context, karma is not created. Consequences are not created.

The habitual pattern of daily life based on desire, dissatisfaction, fear, or attachment is not being supported. It is basically unwinding that part of my nature that in the past would be very pushy about getting things done the way I wanted. By restraining the impulse, the inclination to pushiness is being unwound. So I let someone else come in front in the line. In that moment I am sacrificing my ego's inclination to get ahead.

I am doing something different than what my impulse wants.
I am letting someone go first. My ego is saying, "What are you
doing? You have all these other things you need to do. Today
you are doing the Gita class and you don't have any time." I
neutralize it by taking the opposite action from my inclination.
I assert my authority as a conscious being. That is yogic action.

137. *He has nothing to gain from action nor anything to lose
due to inaction in this world and he does not depend on
anyone for anything.*

Why is this? Because true fulfillment is Self-existent. He
"dwells in the Self, derives satisfaction from the Self." There is
nothing out there that is needed or wanted. I am fulfilled. So
all my acts simply come from what is required, based on what
is before me to do, my dharma.

138. *Therefore, you should always perform your ordained duties
remaining detached. Thus, doing work without attachment,
one can attain the Supreme.*

When you are just beginning this process, this is not likely
to be the case; you are not going to be detached. You are going
to get hooked. And it is going to run its course. You are going
to be depleted and feel like shit, because rajas always leads to
tamas, to inertia. Because you get hooked you will get exhausted
and then move on. At some point you will say, "Argh, I did it
again. I got stuck again. Here I am in the soup being stirred
like everybody else."

You begin to wake up to the fact that this isn't the way
you want to live. This isn't the purpose of your life. This isn't
aligned with the discrimination that has come to you. And you
begin, over time, to move more and more into the right balance
between transcendence and transformation. How much time

do you need to spend in relationship with your inner being, in proportion to the amount of activity engaged in the outer world? What you will notice is that if the transcendence is proportional to the transformation, you will be able to be conscious when you are in the content of your life. But if it is not, then you haven't been meditating or paying attention to your soul enough, and will get overtaken. So the idea of detached action is a goal, but it is also a symptom. It is a symptom of what happens when you spend enough time connected to yourself as the soul.

It is not wrong to be attached to the outcome of your action. It is not wrong to find yourself with an expectation and be disappointed with an outcome. It is just the condition. If you beat yourself up and say, "I must be an awful yogi, I am so attached to the outcome," then you are just feeding the same thing again and creating more karma. The only way you can come out of this mess is by transcendence, by knowing yourself as the soul. Although in this chapter the Gita is speaking about bringing transcendence of the Self into life, it is a continuous process. Over time, over the chapters of the Gita, transcendence will transform us, and it will become more and more natural, even while you are in the midst of the nontranscendent state.

MAINTAINING WORLD ORDER

141. *Arjuna, there is nothing for Me to do in the three worlds nor is there anything worth attaining for Me, yet I am always working.*

What is the duty of an awakened being? What is the relationship of a wise man to an unwise world? How should we be and act? What is our purpose? I have spoken before about the principle of maintaining world order. Why maintain world order? It is so that nature can fulfill its evolutionary purpose. And why does nature need our help with this? Because without the help of transcended beings, nature gets overtaken by the error of the evolutionary process and goes into dissolution and chaos. So when a transcendent being chooses to come back into the world and take yogic action, it lifts nature and gives it the strength of consciousness to continue to follow its evolutionary purpose.

142. *If I cease to work, great harm will occur because men always follow Me in all matters.*
143. *If I cease to work, these worlds will perish and I shall be the cause of confusion and destruction.*

Paraphrasing Krishna, who is fully enlightened, "Even though I am completely fulfilled and there is nothing I need from this world at all, I choose to come into this condition in order to support nature's evolutionary purpose. What I do or don't do affects the collective actualization of truth consciousness on the planet. If I pretend it doesn't make any difference, then nature gets overtaken."

There is the old adage that all man has to do in order for evil to prevail is not to act. So the transcended being that stays in nirvana is not supporting the Mother—the Divine Mother that allowed you to get to nirvana in the first place! It is not fulfilling the very material base that allowed you to wake up to the truth of "what" you are. Therefore, Krishna is saying that even though He is fully enlightened, He comes to this dimension and takes action thanklessly, without expectation, in order to support the Mother in her purpose to bring forward the higher capacities of nature. We are all interconnected. We are all in the oneness. When one part of us comes to a higher state of consciousness, we all get closer to the Sat, the source of the Original Intent.

144. *The unwise always act with attachment; however, the wise man should also always act, but without attachment, in order to ensure the maintenance of world order.*

The act of one who has transcended is much more powerful and has a much greater impact than one who is still invested in the content of life. Since we are all interconnected, for a transcendent being not to take action is to allow the world to devolve, to fall to a lower level. Not to act when action is needed is a form of selfishness. This is why individuals who have come to nirvana, who may live in a cave or stay in an ashram, are pulled to come back to the world this life or in the future. They have an inherent responsibility to support the Mother and the evolutionary intent of this Creation that allowed them to come to that state of consciousness. They have to come back and fulfill that service, that dharma, before it completes.

Krishna is saying that although transcendence is important, yogic action is the means by which transcendence can be completely fulfilled. Through transcendent action you will be bringing something of this transcendence into the world. You will be lifting the condition in which you found yourself into a higher vibration, automatically, just by being connected to the soul.

This then changes the game plan. There will come a time when there is no need for transcendence anymore. There doesn't have to be transcendence and nontranscendence. They start integrating. You come to the place where both states of consciousness coexist. This is what Krishna represents—this integrated state where you know concurrently you are an individual, a person, an ego, and also you are the universe, the vast awareness, the infinity. You are universal and individual, impersonal and personal—at the same time.

This yoga is not just for one's own liberation; it is for the world. It is for all creation. We make a difference in this process because we are all interconnected. When we act or don't act, we are affecting each other. But we are affecting each other most powerfully as we transcend and move closer to truth. As we come closer to the soul, as the source of every living being, then the sacrifices we make benefit more people, many of whom are not capable of making that sacrifice themselves. Jesus Christ sacrificed for mankind by going through the ordeal that he went through, in order to lift the collective consciousness. He made the sacrifice mankind was not capable of. This is the possibility that the Gita is pointing to, right at this early stage of the journey. Maintenance of world order is the sacrifice of the divine being.

TEACHING BY EXAMPLE

145. *A wise man should guide the ignorant by himself, performing action in detachment instead of creating confusion in their minds . . .*
148. *The man of perfect knowledge should not confuse the minds of those who are completely identified with the gunas.*

In these verses the Gita is saying, don't try to teach others how to behave, or tell them how they should fix themselves. Rather teach by your example, by doing it yourself, by being a demonstration. The capacity to act and sacrifice creates a quality of nobility in the soul that automatically evokes respect or admiration from others. We recognize this in a noble soul. We recognize they are not just living for themselves but for others or for a higher good. When there is that kind of recognition, then one is learning through example.

When I saw a photo of my first teacher, Meher Baba, on the wall of a commune, I was an indulgent and rebellious nineteen years old. I saw maturity, patience, and love in his face. He had brought forward through his yogic action a quality of nobility that even an idiot like me could see. I recognized that this is where I wanted to go, not where I was. We teach through the quality of our being, not just through what is taught. We teach through what we are. We make a difference for our children by doing what we want our children to do. We are the example. We change the world through our sacrifice. We change the world through the willingness to become our highest Self, to step out of identification with our human conditioning and by acting for the highest good.

Don't confuse people by having a conversation with them when they are still locked into self-interest, finding benefit or avoiding loss for themselves. Don't bother. If they can't see nobility, then you have no role with them anyway. If you try to teach when there is no listening, it is just wasting energy, or worse, creating karma. It is best to let it be. Otherwise it is just more of what everyone else is doing.

Yet it can be appropriate to teach when someone comes to a certain stage of the journey. This is when the Gita was revealed to Arjuna. When someone comes to the stage of Arjuna—where they are dejected, yet have enough discrimination to know that they are lost and don't know what to do, but they are open— then knowledge of this teaching can make a big difference. It can help them begin the journey. This is the purpose of the Gita. It shows a way to live, and teach it by living it, by being it. Living it leads to integration, to integrity. Only those who know themselves as the soul can be a demonstration of this truth. Only they are capable of great sacrifices. Only those who have reached a place of detachment and freedom from pain, pleasure, preferences, repulsions, and attractions can bear the sacrifices that lift mankind.

THE PULL OF ATTRACTION AND REPULSION

149. *With your mind fixed on Me, the Supreme Self, Arjuna, dedicate all your actions to Me and be free from attachment and desire; thus, freeing yourself from grief, fight the battle.*

In this verse Krishna is giving Arjuna a means of going beyond attachment to the outcome of our action. The secret is to live for the divine, to have all your acts be a sacrifice for the divine.

152. *All beings, even the wise, follow their innate nature; how far can one go with external restraint only?*

153. *Attraction and repulsion are rooted in the senses for their objects. One should never be a victim of these two because they are formidable enemies on the path of yoga.*

154. *Your own path, even if devoid of apparent merits, is better than others that appear to you to be easy. It is better to face death while pursuing your own path than to follow another's path; it may be fraught with danger.*

These verses reinforce what I have been talking about. The last two verses give a little additional information about the pull of attraction and repulsion. The structures of attraction and repulsion are linked to our senses and are all-pervasive. They are what pull us this way or push us that way, causing us to be like a dog wagged by its tail. They keep us in bondage. Our attractions cause us to seek outside ourselves for our fulfillment. Our repulsions cause us to avoid, withdraw, and isolate, to pull back from things outside of ourselves. This keeps us stuck in the existing condition of our life.

The key idea is to be able to have your attractions equal your repulsions; to be able to be with your repulsions with equal ease as your attractions, and not to make decisions or act based on either. There is no sin in attraction and repulsion except our desire or fear: our desire for what we are attracted to, and our fear of what we are repulsed by. This is what keeps us limited, in a state of bondage.

If you notice yourself being repulsed, then move toward that repulsion. If you have someone difficult in your life, take their picture, put them on your altar, and stay present with what role they have in your life. Notice the repulsion. Enter into it. To choose to enter into repulsion is a yogic act. It is a sacrifice because you are doing what you don't want to do. The Brahman manifests when you do this. Your consciousness automatically

THE BHAGAVAD GITA REVEALED

lifts when you meet that which you are repulsed by. You will begin to see the nature of repulsion and begin to realize that there is no repulsion except in yourself. Put these people on your altar until you are able to be with them in neutrality, acceptance, forgiveness, or love. Then you have unwound that particular inclination. This is yogic action.

If you notice yourself being attracted to something where you have got to have it but instead you restrain yourself, this is also a yogic act. Instead of acting on your inclination, instead of trying to possess it or cling to it, step back. Be present with the fire that this brings up. Watch the attraction pull at you like a frenzy. What happens when we don't get what we want? Especially when we really want it? A fire comes up; anger comes up. That is when you begin to dissolve desire and anger. You are meeting your rajas, burning it out of your system.

Verse 153 gives a whole arena in which to work with yogic action. Stop avoiding things you don't want to be with. Stop going after things that you do want to be with, that are attractive. Learn to accept being with what you don't want and not having what you want. This teaches you how to accept what you have. Meet the thing you are repulsed by or attracted to without taking action and stay with the process this activates in you. This is your path to freedom from the domination of these two. It is not greener on the other side. Wherever you go, there you are. Don't fool yourself with future imaginings or past longings. Be where you are. Be with what is showing up for you right here, right now. This is the core message of these verses.

DESIRE: THE FORMIDABLE ENEMY

Arjuna asked:

155. *Then what is the force that compels man to commit sin even against his own will?*

The Blessed Lord said:

156. *This is the force of desire and anger that comes out of rajas.
It is powerful, extremely harmful, and it is the real enemy.*
157. *As fire is covered by smoke and mirror is covered by dust, as
an embryo is enveloped by the membrane, so also knowledge
is covered by desire and anger.*
158. *Arjuna, wisdom is covered by this eternal enemy we call
desire. It is like insatiable fire.*

Here, in these last verses of Chapter 3, Krishna is pointing
to the real problem, the task before you. Action that arises from
rajas creates desire, and desire creates anger. You get caught
and completely absorbed in the mechanism of these. You are
immediately veiled from your capacity to know the truth. If
you really want something and don't get it, you become frustrated. Then watch: You will see delusion run its number. You
will get swept away by desire and its bedfellows—frustration,
resentment, anger, and hatred.

This is the real enemy, the Gita is saying. It will smash
you. It will destroy your ability to access yourself for a period
of time, although not forever. But if you don't have the right
information about how this process works, it may be a long time.
You can come out of it relatively quickly if you are engaged in
conscious yogic action.

At the end of Chapter 2 the Gita talked about the nature
of the fall in Verses 109 and 110, where the attachment to the
senses comes when one's consciousness dwells on sense objects.
Becoming attached to having what you want is dwelling on the
sense object. And once you get attached, there is desire. The
more you focus on it, the more you want it! And if you can't
get it, you become frustrated and angry. And with anger comes
delusion. Delusion veils your physical, your vital, and your
mental components. You lose the ability to discriminate. You

are caught up in an obsession. You can't step back and get any distance. It sucks you in. You are in the whirlwind.

This is probably Krishna's strongest statement in the Gita. The real enemy is this passion, this force of desire and anger that comes out of rajas. Rajas, the impulse for action, binds us. These moments are the real tests, the real battle. It can thwart our ability to progress on the spiritual path. This desire and anger sucks us into the drama that comes from the vital drives. These overtake us and smash us against the shores of *samskara*. The repercussions go on and on.

160. *Therefore, you must control your senses and kill this powerful enemy that covers truth and wisdom.*

In order to control this rajas Krishna says, *"You must control your senses."* Indulging in the object of the senses—what you hear, see, feel, taste, or smell—feeds impulsiveness and reactivity. Only if you can retrain them can you gain enough authority not to be overtaken. It is like a coiled spring that gets triggered. If you have low tolerance for being frustrated, then you will react. You become a tantruming child, a raging adult. "If I can't get what I want, I don't care about you or anything else." This immature reaction has consequences; it creates karma. It binds our consciousness.

This desire and anger that comes out of rajas is the real challenge. Like many Westerners, Arjuna's vital is very strong. Our whims and wants have been indulged. We feel we should get what we want. This has weakened us. So it is harder to break this pattern when we come to the spiritual path. When our spiritual seeking is motivated by desire, we get overtaken by rajas. We become impatient and don't feel we are making progress, or angry because things are not the way we want them. We become frustrated, disillusioned, angry, and resentful. We convert the very thing that frees us from anger and desire into another way to bind ourselves. So we have to be alert. We have to be present to recognize this pattern in ourselves.

161. *Senses are said to be more powerful than the body, but greater than the senses is the mind, superior to the mind is the intellect, and superior to the intellect is the Self.*

Krishna says above, *"Senses are said to be more powerful than the body."* Why is that? The body, if it didn't have the senses, would not know of existence. The senses bring the signals of life to us. They tell the body if something is sharp, or hard, if this will hurt, or if something feels good. So the senses rule the body. And what rules the senses? The mind. It says, "If I eat too much of this, I am not going to feel good." So my mind says not to eat too much. When I exercise I feel good, so the mind says, "OK, I will exercise." So the mind can rule the senses.

"And superior to the mind is the intellect." The intellect has a purpose higher than fulfilling the push or pull of the senses. When you set a goal for yourself through the intellect, you expand your focus and start making something more important than sensory fulfillment. This helps us go beyond the way the mind has ruled things up to that point. We come out of the old, small, familiar paradigm and step into a larger paradigm. The intellect has this ability to sense another possibility than the current one you are living; it has the ability to step out of your existing point of view. It allows you to expand, to learn, and to grow.

We all have gone through this process in our lives. We came out of elementary school where we were on the top rung and went to high school where we were on the bottom rung. Such is life. We learn that we have to manage our lower nature through our intellect in order to get along or get what we want out of life. We learn to endure calmly. So the intellect helps us transcend our lower nature in certain situations.

162. *Therefore, Arjuna, knowing that which is superior to the intellect, control your mind through reasoning and kill the formidable enemy called desire.*

But once we turn to the spiritual path, that which is still more powerful than the intellect is the soul. The soul pulls us to something larger than ourselves, gives us the strength and aspiration to know our true, divine nature. Once that happens, all the other subsequent layers of yourself follow more quickly. While the intellect can control the senses more powerfully than the mind, the soul—or Self—can control the senses more powerfully than the intellect. Know yourself as the soul. Then you will automatically control your senses. Abide in what you are as a being, as the soul, and automatically your senses will moderate their ability to influence you, shape you, or run you. That is the secret of Chapter 3. In the next chapter Krishna takes us out of this battle and shows us how to move into a more profound relationship to the soul, to the Self.

CHAPTER 4

The Yoga of Knowledge

*After attaining the supreme knowledge you will not be deluded
and through that knowledge you will realize that this entire
creation is within you and you are in Me.*

~ VERSE 197

L et us begin by looking at the relevance of this chapter in
terms of the journey in which the soul has been engaged
up to this point. We started with dejection. We came out of
dejection with discrimination, even if only in the mental plane.
We set a trajectory on the path of conscious action. We began
to put our discrimination into action—making changes in our
lives consistent with what has taken us out of the ocean of
dejection. This is bringing some peace and a sense of purpose.

The more our actions are aligned with this movement, the
more quickly they are reinforced. Then what you are seeking
begins to be revealed to you in an indescribable way. It's as if
you connect to that which is seeking you at the same time you
are seeking it. You get in touch with something within. This
is the beginning of the Yoga of Knowledge.

Soul Contact Brings Knowledge

The term for knowledge in Sanskrit is *jñana*, which means direct knowledge of the soul. It is not the knowledge of mind that is gained through learning and experience in the worldly life. The knowledge we speak of here does not begin until there is some contact with that inexplicable quality of our essential being, or soul. This can be accessed in the expansiveness of your awareness in the mental plane or in your heart or body. It is felt as a sense of peace or connection. Both give strength and direction. When this contact becomes more prevalent, then the motive gets stronger, and the actions become more effective, and the direction more intuitive. We get pulled to some things, pushed away from others.

Once we experience this soul contact we want whatever brings more of that. We get less attracted to that which is contrary to it. Some symptoms could be a loss of interest in going to bars, or talking about sports, or watching a lot of TV, or playing hours of video games. Something just feels as if it has had enough. Dissatisfaction with these diversions increases. They no longer bring the fulfillment they once did. Something else is calling. Something else is pulling. You begin reading spiritual books, going to seminars, developing yourself. A sense of value becomes more poignant. This is what the yoga of action is pointing to—"that" in us which recognizes what leads to soul contact and what does not.

As in Chapter 2, we are becoming more capable of discriminating what is real from what is unreal but without necessarily thinking about it. There is an innate dissatisfaction at this state, an innate discomfort with life as it is. That dissatisfaction pushes you to keep seeking, to keep changing. These soul contacts begin to accumulate, and you gain a strength that becomes more and more available.

For example, you take up meditation. At first you just find yourself sitting there with your thoughts, dissatisfied, wishing you could be elsewhere. When it is over you are not sure if you will come back, but you do. The next time you sit, you notice something happening, but you don't know what. So you come back again and something starts opening up. You find some quiet. Your thoughts are not so noisy. There is a sense of value, which feeds your motivation and builds your reservoir of truth.

You are strengthening a capacity to go forward. This is what the Yoga of Knowledge is about. It is about acquiring contact, connection, and awareness with "that" which is bringing you nurturance, purpose, and fulfillment. You could do this for many years. Many people are wandering between Chapters 3 and 4, not sure where they are going. Their personal lives are still filled with responsibilities, worries, addictions, and habits. At this point the new awareness is intermingled with the rest of life. The value is not so apparent.

But with the Yoga of Knowledge, a momentum grows. There is now a need to do the spiritual thing. Without it you become miserable. It becomes more important and takes on more value. It moves up your list of priorities. Slowly the importance of making contact becomes a greater priority. The Gita points out that gaining knowledge is a slow process of unfolding revelation, and it comes because of the previous efforts that we have wittingly or unwittingly taken toward truth.

Let's move into Chapter 4, The Yoga of Knowledge (Jñana Yoga).

THE STAGES OF REVELATION

The Blessed Lord said:

163. *I taught this imperishable yoga first to Vivaswan, the god of light, he taught it to Manu, and Manu imparted it to Ikshvaku.*

164. *Thus it was transferred in succession and came to the royal sages. But due to the impact of time this eternal union was lost to mankind.*

165. *I am revealing this supreme secret path of yoga to you since you are My devotee and companion.*

In this introduction Krishna is saying that although this supreme secret path of yoga has been around forever, it gets revealed in stages. Truth, or Sat, was first received by the psychic awareness known as Vivaswan. Then it went to Manu, the mind. Just as the sun is the source of light but the moon reflects its light, so is the Sat the source of light, and Manu, the mind, the intelligence, reflects this truth as knowledge. It gives us self-awareness, the ability to understand and learn. These are not the Sat itself, but its reflection. From the mind it went to the vital, or Ikshyaku, the emotional nature and the drives. Over time this truth descended into the human system, into the vital layer until it came to the royal sages. They were able to bring it into their lives and bodies through their day-to-day actions.

The Gita is teaching a path that brings truth to all parts of our nature: not just the psychic, or the intelligence, or the mind, or the emotional nature, but to the actual physical nature and into the way we live and act. This is the uniqueness of this revelation of the Gita.

In the third verse Krishna says, "I am revealing this supreme secret path of yoga to you since you are My devotee and companion." This will not be revealed unless you are seeking in some way. It will not be shown unless you have aspiration, devotion, a pull toward truth. To begin this journey, an aspiration for something more real and true is necessary. An attitude of seeking is the prerequisite for this, the first of multiple revelations that occur in the Gita.

The "Yoga of Complaining"

Arjuna said:

166. *Vivaswan, the god of light, was born before you. How is it that you taught this yoga to him at the beginning?*

This revelation begins with Arjuna saying, "Wait a second. You are standing before me now. How could you have been here at the origin?" He is still in his mind, his programmed self, and is saying, "I don't understand this." He is complaining again as he was in the beginning of the third chapter. Complaining is usually a constant companion to the seeker. There should be a yoga of complaining! It is always the entry point in which the teacher moves into relationship with the seeker. As long as there is sincerity, the teacher will give space for complaining because it is a way of coming to clarification.

The Blessed Lord said:

167. *Arjuna, you and I both have passed through many births. I have remembered all of them but you have forgotten them.*

How did Krishna explain this to Arjuna? He said, "I have remembered all my births. We've always been together. You just don't remember, but I remember every one." He is saying that this process in which they are engaged goes on and on eternally. He points to the continuity of the soul. The soul can take birth and death and birth and death and yet something remembers. This something is the string on which all these lives are the beads. As we come to a certain state of consciousness, the ability to access what you are, what you have been, and what you will always be, is part of the process of coming to the truth of what you are. There is a continuity of consciousness.

KRISHNA'S CLOAK

168. *Although I am unborn and immutable, I manifest Myself through My own maya by keeping My prakriti under control.*

Krishna then reveals something of his nature. These next verses contain important concepts. "Although I am unborn and immutable, I manifest Myself through My own *maya* by keeping My *prakriti* under control." There are two new terms here. The first is maya, which is the apparentness of things. It includes illusion and delusion. It is that which appears to be real but which is not. He is saying that He manifests Himself by putting on the cloak of appearance. In this way He can be seen; if Krishna didn't wear this cloak, Arjuna would not know He was there.

In Chapter 3 Krishna said He had no reason to manifest except for the purpose of maintaining world order. So He is restating this. He is manifesting by keeping His prakriti under control. What is prakriti? It is our personality: our mind, thoughts, beliefs, opinions, drives, wants, and preferences. Prakriti is also our affections, attachments, desires, and hopes, as well as our body, sensations, attractions, and repulsions. It is what animates all that exists. For each of us it is our personality, the content of our mental, vital and physical nature. It is the Tat. And the *purusha* is the context in which the content arises, that which has no content or attributes. Prakriti is the content and the veil of appearances.

Krishna is saying that He wears this cloak consciously and has it under control. He is speaking from the fully realized state, one who has come and rests in the consciousness of the soul, and yet continues to function in the world in a masterful way with greater and greater capacity to control the personality. Prakriti quiets when the soul takes full possession of an individual being. The prakriti begins to organize itself around the being. This is evidence of true transformation. The soul enters more fully into the person, and in the process the person changes. The soul integrates the knowledge that descends through all the different planes. Your prakriti, which is what the soul is descending into, transforms in the process.

THE PROMISE OF THE AVATAR

169. *Whenever the light of natural law fades away and there is an ascendancy of darkness, during those periods I create Myself.*
170. *For the protection of the virtuous, to destroy evil, and to reestablish dharma, I come again and again.*

Here Krishna speaks of why He comes. "Whenever the light of natural law fades away and there is an ascendancy of darkness, during those periods I create Myself." In the course of our lives and in the course of humanity's evolution, there are periods of darkness. In these periods of darkness consciousness becomes so dissatisfied, so miserable, that a cry arises. Out of dejection comes aspiration. Out of these periods of darkness, the Krishna in us comes forward. The divine in us cries out, asking to be released from darkness, to be free from its unwitting attachment that is causing this obscurity.

"I come again and again, whenever there is an ascendancy of darkness." This points to two things in the Gita. First it is the principle of the *avatar*, which in the Vedic tradition Krishna represents. An avatar comes to the world periodically to help lift the collective humankind out of a particular slump or to help the collective consciousness move into a new era, which is where we are right now. We are being lifted into a new level of consciousness, which is bringing forward a new era, one aspect of which is the manifestation of the avatar coming for the whole world.

We also see this new level of consciousness as it manifests in each of us as we experience the cycles of the gunas. These cycles are the veils that distort our ability to know and experience reality directly, as it is. They pervade all human dynamics. In the normal course of human life these gunas come up in certain predictable cycles. In my experience they are six-, nine-, or twelve-year cycles. Within those cycles one comes out of tamas, ascends into sattwa, expands into rajas, then exhausts itself, returning to tamas and so on, endlessly.

At the universal and individual level there is this descent into darkness and coming out again. The individual comes out of tamas bringing forward the sattwa, the inner Krishna, the divinity within, the light of knowledge coming back to reclaim the kingdom that has been forgotten. Krishna describes this process here: "For the protection of the virtuous, to destroy evil, and to reestablish dharma, I come again and again." Here are listed the three qualities of the divine awakening, the three aspects of spiritual awakening.

First, is the strengthening of virtue, strengthening the light of the soul. The innate purity of our unconditioned Self is strengthened, as well as our ability to feel and know truth.

Second, is the destruction of evil. I call this the transformation of untruth. It is the changing of what is untrue into what is true. It is not destroying evil per se, but the transmutation of ignorance that perpetuates bondage. It is the transmutation of behaviors or reactions that keep us trapped. In this new cycle we shift to a higher consciousness.

Third, is the reestablishment of dharma—the ability to act and live in alignment with the higher truth. These three follow each other and complete themselves in the dharma. When you learn how to act while aligned with higher truth, virtue is strengthened and evil is destroyed. This in turn reestablishes your ability to live in alignment with truth, which further strengthens virtue and destroys non-virtue. This capacity to move from truth to higher truth is a process of realizing untruth at progressively deeper and deeper levels. This process creates a natural ascending spiral that comes again and again.

MANY PATHS, ONE GOAL

171. *Arjuna, whosoever knows the mystery of My divine birth and divine action is not reborn after death but attains Me.*
172. *Being free from attachment, fear, and anger, and keeping Me constantly in their minds through pursuing the path of pure knowledge, many have attained Me.*
173. *Whichever path men may follow to reach Me, I grant their prayer. Men always follow My path.*

Here Krishna is pointing to the universality of all paths. All paths actually strive for the same goal. What is a path? It is not Buddhism or Hinduism or any specific religion. It is something each of us walks in our own way. But it is not a straight line for most. We become diverted where instead of continuing to grow, we get caught up or distracted by lesser truths, or stop to enjoy what is attained. Initially those paths will not take us to the same goal, but we eventually end up discovering the soul, no matter how waylaid we get. The only difference is time.

The Gita is pointing to universality, to the basic fundamental truths to be found in all paths. That is why it says in the second chapter, "Even a little knowledge of this path is sufficient to free you from great fear." The sense of progress is tangible. While others wander in different directions following whims and desires, the Gita sets a trajectory. It provides an intellectual understanding so that all of one's actions will eventually come into alignment with it. When Krishna says, "This is My path," he is speaking from the fully enlightened, realized state of consciousness. This is the realization that will come as soon as we quit being so invested in keeping our egos in place. When we stop ego-ing, we become the soul.

The great thing about this knowledge is that it is always right here, right now. When you get rid of everything else, there is nothing for you to do or make happen, because the right action is right here, right now. It's so simple, so plain, so ordinary. Yet the ego cannot tolerate that vacuum. It cannot tolerate living in the state of the soul. It is so habituated to striving, creating endless instability, yet always seeking stability. The ego doesn't know that by rejecting this striving it would find stability. The instability is due to our identification with the content of our lives, the story, the personality, the inclinations—all the forces that have shaped us into this separated state.

"Whichever path men may follow to reach Me, I grant their prayer." Instead of *follow*, let's use the word *aspire*. Once you aspire to perceive reality, to perceive truth, then you begin a process of enlightenment. The direct perception of truth is knowledge. That is what is being talked about here. The perception of what is "real" or "true"—which the Gita calls the soul, or the atman—is the knowledge of what is right here, right now, eternally unchanging. As soon as you aspire, as soon as you have the prayer, the path comes to you. Then no matter what you do, as long as you remember the prayer, as long as you stay in touch with your aspiration to know what is real or true, everything you do is walking the path.

This is the power of "intention" that arises from prayer, from aspiration. It creates a new paradigm for existence other than the one based on the little, mean, grasping, defensive, fearful ego. It doesn't get diverted by thinking happiness is over here, or happiness is over there. With true intention you can't step off this path. No matter how you live, as long as you are in touch with your prayer—or as the Gita says, "as long as you think of Me"—you will find your way. You keep recovering the prayer because what is praying in you, what is aspiring in you, is the same as that which you are seeking.

The more you are in touch with the aspiration and the prayer, the forward-reaching movement in your being, then the more you experience your unconditional nature, and the more you un-condition your soul. All paths lead to the same goal—the atman, the soul, the piece of the Absolute that lies within each of us. Every prayer, every aspiration is a unique path. Each person travels a unique journey, shaped by the characteristics and qualities they were born with.

ASPIRATION AND THE FOURFOLD ORDER

175. *On the basis of man's innate nature and tendencies for action I have created the fourfold order in this world, but I, the Imperishable, am always a non-doer.*

The Vedas and the Bhagavad Gita say all of mankind is clustered into four major castes. Each person in each of these castes has an innate nature that determines his or her role or capacity, his or her unique dharma or approach to the world and the spiritual path. Let's just pretend there are 2,500 different possible human personalities, like 2,500 models of cars. And you are born into one of those. You become identified with what you were born into. You think you are one two-thousand-five-hundredth of all those possible human personalities. You become that personality. When someone else gets born into that same human personality model in another part of the world, although they may look differently and speak a different language, they have the same personality. They think the way you think, they react the way you react, and they think they are that. But once you wake up and come out of your identification with that personality model, just like coming out of a car, you remember that you are the driver. You have a vehicle that you drive, but you are not the vehicle.

I see that this pattern of identification with one's personality is perpetuated through one's ancestral karmas. The body is the product of the union of a mother and a father. And they are each products of the union of their parents and so on. Each family line is a branch of the entire collection of possible personality types. We all carry a little bit of everybody in each of us. We are the distillations of inclinations and propensities and tendencies that have come from the collective consciousness of mankind and that have found expression in a vehicle. The vehicle carries not just a physical inclination, but also an emotional and energetic inclination, and likes and dislikes. It carries a certain way of thinking and knowing.

The Vedas group these different characteristics into clusters. The Sudras are tamasic, the most simple and ordinary kind of people. They tend to be very material and don't need much to be happy. They enjoy their lives and don't think much about things. They love their comforts and pleasures—sitting at home, drinking a beer, watching TV. They are embodied tamas.

Then there are the Vaishyas. They are like the sudras but always in action, rajasic, ambitious, and wanting things. They are business people who calculate how to improve their situation, control their lives, and get more of what they want. The Vaishyas are always in negotiation with life. They are always calculating and figuring out the cost-benefit ratio of their relationships, their job, their house, the people in their lives. The Vaishya is the rajas coming out of tamas.

Next are the Kshatriyas. They are rajasic, but have sattwic aspirations. They are the warriors, the inspirers, the initiators. They take on causes and undertakings without personal benefit. They are able to make sacrifices that don't give immediate fulfillment. They are the politicians, the activists, the creative people, the idealists. They strive to improve the world or themselves. This is rajas moving toward sattwa.

Then there are the Brahmins. They are primarily sattwic: they are keepers of the wisdom of mankind, the priests, monks, teachers and philosophers, artists, poets, the saints and divine beings. They bring light, love and truth to the world, although they are not always aware of it.

Each personality type, each person as they evolve in life moves higher and higher in vibration, from tamas to rajas to sattwa. But each part of one's nature may evolve differently. There might be part of you that is more like a Sudra, part of you that is more like a Kshatriya, and part of you that is more like a Brahmin. In sum total, we tend to cluster somewhere in these four categories, from a lower vibration to a higher vibration. The path of a Sudra would be different from the path of a Brahmin. The path of a Vaishyas, the businessman, would be different than the path of a Kshatriyas, a warrior who is striving to bring in something new.

Within these categories we each have a unique spiritual path to travel, even if the structures are the same. As long as there is prayer, we will continue to travel. As long as there is aspiration, we will move along the path. If aspiration is forgotten there is no movement. It becomes like water flowing off a mountain from a snowmelt heading toward the ocean, but then it reaches an open plain. The water quits moving and becomes stagnant. It doesn't reach the goal of the ocean. This can be true of all paths. Aspiration keeps us moving.

Our ability to be in touch with our aspiration, with our prayer, takes us to the completion of this journey from human existence to divine existence. Without this there is no current, no motor, no capacity to travel. You just swirl around, bouncing against the shores, caught in the swamps and eddies of life, accumulating more and more debris, becoming heavier and heavier, covered with seaweed. This is the nature of the journey if you are not moving. You gather moss and barnacles. Even if the current picks up, you don't move much. You are scraping along the bottom. It is only this aspiration that keeps you from losing momentum and becoming inert.

ACTION IN INACTION, INACTION IN ACTION

178. *As to what is action and what is inaction, even the wise men are confused. Therefore, I shall reveal to you the truth about action and this knowledge will free you from the evils of action.*
179. *The effects of action are profound; therefore, one should know what is action, what is inaction, and what is prohibited action.*

Now we are getting into the meat of this chapter. What is action? What is inaction? And what is prohibited action? Action binds you, inaction is neutral, and prohibited action binds you aggressively. Action was revealed in Chapter 3 as a means to truth. However, if done with a desire motive or an attachment to the outcome, action is likely to perpetuate bondage: the patterns, preferences, and inclinations of your old nature. So there are actions that we take because of our programming that will continue to reinforce the programming. For example, every time you complain and want it different than it is, every time you desire something or hang onto something, you are just adding to your bondage. When you act or react based on those inclinations, you are just adding more baggage or karma, the consequences of previous actions.

When we stop acting based on our programming, then the effort not to act is inaction. Inaction stops the accumulation of that particular cluster of inclinations or samskaras, those drives or tendencies toward types of actions. When you restrain the action, then for as long as you are not acting, you are not adding to the baggage; you begin to unwind the rope of inclinations.

In addition, there are prohibited actions, those that tighten the ropes that bind you to your identity as a separate personality. Lust, greed, and anger are examples of prohibited actions, as are becoming addicted, going into a rage, or feeding a self-destructive inclination. Prohibited actions strongly reinforce the pattern of accumulating bondage.

Yet when we come to a state of "actionlessness," then all acts we take undo the inclination to act. Actionlessness was revealed in Chapter 3, and now we are expanding on it. At this stage when we act, we are simultaneously in touch with truth. Only the baggage of untruth prevents us from knowing this more deeply. Once we undo the baggage, we reveal what has been there all along. To come to what you are in truth is always a process of subtraction: a process of undoing, of letting go of behaviors and thoughts that perpetuate suffering.

So how do you unwind these ties that bind? You unwind them by acting in ways aligned with the truth of what you are. Your acts are consistent with your aspiration, your prayer. Your acts are consistent with your willingness to sacrifice everything that still binds you. You give up your preferences and self-defeating thinking, acting, and speaking that has been running you. You become willing to sacrifice your bondage—that to which you are attached and think is you. Letting go of baggage is actionlessness. It is not necessary that you consciously stop behaving the way you are inclined, but rather that you have an intention, an aspiration in every situation to be in truth, to be in the correct relationship to existence, to be in the prayer. This is the attitude one develops.

You should know something else about bondage. It is the accumulation of baggage that creates "who" you are, the personality. It is this "who" that doesn't want change. It is this "who" that is perpetuating habits. You can't imagine giving up these things because they are what define you, give you a sense of worth, or protect you, or get you what you want. You are so tangled in it that the very thing that is veiling you from the truth of yourself is what defines who you are. Unwittingly you keep reinvesting in the individual self. "I am my personality. I am my thoughts. Don't dare tell me otherwise. I am right. I have to be right. I'm afraid that if I am wrong I would die. If I am wrong I am defeated, I am less, and to be less is frightening."

To be diminished, to be less—yet that is the very pathway that takes us to freedom. This is what is being described in this chapter. How do you organize yourself so that you can begin to act true from within your bondage? You are only just catching on that your actions make a difference. The word "karma" indicates both the consequences of previous action and that which reinforces the inclination for action. Action creates action. Karma creates karma. You take an action and there is a consequence. This consequence is much bigger than you know. Why? Because we are all inter-connected. This whole manifested creation is a tapestry of interconnecting components of which each of us is a node. And what we do or don't do affects the entire collective. Everything we do or don't do has a consequence for good, ill, or neutral.

Every time we move we are setting things off, whether we know it or not. We become immune to these consequences. Like a bull in a china shop, we become oblivious to them, mind-lessly knocking tea cups this way and that, sending fragments flying. We are the same way. We are in a minefield. Every action has consequences, and these consequences have an impact, a karma that weighs us down. If it is not undoing or neutral, we are feeding the inclinations that have us performing acts that keep us bound.

By understanding that actions have consequences, and experiencing the consequences, you learn. But if you are not aware of the consequences of your actions, then you can't learn. You don't know why everything is going wrong. You are just driving down the road looking in the rearview mirror, and it seems like everybody is crashing into you. What is the problem? Your orientation is in error. Your attitude is the error. You are completely a victim of your own ignorance, with no capacity to learn. This is ignorance, and ignorance is bondage. We are all in bondage, even at this moment, even those with some degree of enlightenment. We are all in bondage until the final threshold is crossed. When you can see your bondage and where you are free, then you are truly a wise being.

ACTIONS THAT FREE

181. *One who is able to perform actions without a desire motive and whose actions are sanctified by the fire of knowledge is fit to be called a sage.*
182. *One who is not attached to the fruits of action, is ever satisfied and no longer depends on others, really does nothing even though fully engaged in action.*
183. *A person who has controlled his mind and body, is free from desire, and has given up possessions and sense enjoyment does not incur sin but performs actions through the body only.*

These verses describe the technology behind the Yoga of Knowledge and give specific directions about the different types of acts that free you. The first principle is that acts done as a sacrifice or offering to that which is greater than yourself, will be free of self-interest. Any time you don't allow the reactions or inclinations of your body to control you, or those of your mind, or emotions, you are offering these up. In time, these acts of offering undo these inclinations, and increase your ability to access the truth of what you are. If there is a light bulb inside a skein of yarn, the more yarn that you unwind, the more light peeks through and the more luminous the yarn becomes. Knowledge comes through the subtraction of the inclinations that keep the yarn accumulating.

"One who is not attached to the fruits of action . . ." You become aware that you are attached to the fruits of action when you get frustrated or angry when things don't go your way. You can know that your investment is causing suffering. You can know that your expectations are making you miserable. A process reveals itself through the struggle to let go, to detach: the struggle to accept what is occurring, rather than wanting it to be different. In that struggle, you begin to undo the inclinations to those acts, and that which will allow true satisfaction with what arises reveals itself.

"A person who has controlled his mind . . ." How many of you have controlled your mind? Thoughts go on and on. It is the inclination of the mind to create thoughts. We have strongly fed this active thinking in our culture. We have it wound up tightly. We have a lot of coiled springs wired up in thinking. Even if you make much progress on the spiritual path, this wound-up habit of thinking still has a lot of energy locked up in it. Learning how to be present with the ever-whirling thought structure is difficult and very tedious. You first become aware of your thoughts. Then you learn to endure them without acting on them. This is a form of suffering. You are your thoughts and do not know how much you are suffering. Once you become aware of your thoughts, you begin to realize how much thinking is suffering, how painful it is to be dissatisfied, to have an opinion, expectation, or judgment.

When you become aware of what is running you, you begin to undo the inclination to continue feeding this. But even so, it takes time, because of the previous karma that you have accumulated. You are going to have to endure the process calmly as it unwinds. You are going to have to learn how to be in the fire of actionlessness, to be present with it so that the energy can unwind. As it unwinds, it relaxes. As it relaxes, the mind grows quieter; you have more space between thoughts. This same kind of winding has also occurred in every part of our system: our feelings, our desires, our addictions, our physical habits, and our routines.

184. *When one is satisfied with whatever is available without asking, is free from the problem of opposites and jealousy and is balanced in success and failure, then he is not bound by actions.*

185. *One who is free from attachments and has no identification with the body or the mind and is firmly established in knowledge, for whom work is a sacrifice, for such a person all works melt away.*

The Gita is pointing to where this trajectory is going. It is pointing to the symptoms that one begins to manifest when the yoga of knowledge becomes dominant. One becomes less attached to the outcome of action. There is more satisfaction in just being where you are. There is movement away from endless doing, getting, avoiding, and striving. There are more fulfilling moments of quiet without any purpose or direction.

Acts of sacrifice, of changing the old way we have been living based on our inclinations and environment, set the base for a more effective and intentional form of sacrifice. This is the beginning of what we call spiritual practices. This is the beginning of this yoga of knowledge, of conscious effort for the purpose of unveiling and dismantling our habitual old ways and strengthening the new ways of being connected with the truth of our being. Previously this took work. Now, at this stage of the journey, it is starting to be natural.

Seeing Brahman Everywhere

186. *One who aims at the Supreme sees Brahman everywhere, such as in the fire, in the offering, in the oblation, in the goal, and finally in himself.*

This is a complete summary. "One who aims at the Supreme," the truth of ourselves, the truth of the soul, sees the divine in every situation. Your purpose begins to set your trajectory. When you have that trajectory, then you can see how every situation in your life becomes an opportunity to move closer toward your goal. All of life becomes recontextualized because your new intention is to move out of the domain of human satisfaction and ego fulfillment and into another dimension of being. That intention is creating a new way of looking at the world and being in it. Instead of seeing obstacles, you see opportunities. Instead of outward happiness, you find inward fulfillment. You can now see allurement as traps. You begin to discern the world in light of your purpose. You begin to see the Brahman everywhere, and in the process, within yourself.

This is a very important point. We are all, in fact, expressions of the Supreme Being. What the Supreme looks like in this dimension is like nothing. When I was a kid we used to play with papier-mâché. We would blow up a balloon, tie it off, and coat it with strips of newspaper soaked in glue. After we had coated it with enough strips of paper and left it overnight, the paper became solid. We could pop the balloon and the paper form would hold its shape. What was inside was a void. We could keep adding strips of paper and make it into a giraffe or elephant or a mom or dad or a dog. But it held this emptiness, this nothingness, this void.

The void is always there. The Brahman, the truth, the soul in this dimension, looks and feels like a void at first. What allows for the void in the case of a papier-mâché form is air

The Bhagavad Gita Revealed

that is trapped inside the balloon. Even though the form is surrounded by air, air is also trapped inside. If that shell had a personality, then you would have an accurate analogy of our condition. The papier-mâché shell is the "who" we are and the inner void is the "what" we are.

When you look outward you see trees and plants and grass. They are all like papier-mâché creations. They are all animated by this apparent emptiness, which is in fact the original condition of consciousness, the Brahman, the truth of what they are. It is through this void that all of life is animated. When you first begin to see this quality behind all appearances, it may seem to be a glorious radiance, beauty, and harmony in sight and sound. But in fact it is just a reflection of that inner quality of being that you are. You move into relationship with that radiant quality, which is nothing other than the very thing that is seeing it, cloaked in the same kind of papier-mâché creation you mistakenly believe you are.

Finding this quality within yourself is the Yoga of Knowledge. Knowing this quality is different than knowing the papier-mâché world. It has a whole different quality of being; there is no reference point to know what it is by using your papier-mâché mind, or your papier-mâché vital, or your papier-mâché personality. This process of connecting with that which is animating you and everything else may at first be seen outwardly, but ultimately you find it inwardly. Some find it first inwardly before they see it outwardly. This verse points to that. Now we get into the work of burning off the papier-mâché.

SACRIFICING IN THE FIRE OF YOGA

187. *Some yogis sacrifice to gods, others sacrifice the sacrifice itself in the fire of Brahman.*
188. *Others offer senses like hearing, etc., into the fire of self-control; still others offer sound and other objects of the senses in the fire of senses.*

189. *All the functions of the senses and of the vital airs are offered as sacrifice in the fire of yoga by way of self-control by those whose vision is kindled by the fire of knowledge.*

These are the sacrifices. Now let's explore the principle of sacrifice, which is really the offering that was revealed in Chapter 3, and apply it directly to our own perception, our own values, our own issues. We are beginning to come forward and become conscious of the papier-mâché person that we are living. Sacrifice is like peeling off accumulated layers of newspaper: stories, beliefs, memories, and habits. That is the sacrifice. Without sacrifice, those things live us. They wake us up in the morning and have us eat certain foods and act in habitual ways. It is just the machine, the papier-mâché vehicle, the human form that is animated and has its own purpose. Its purpose is to perpetuate itself to survive and succeed. It has nothing to do with you, the occupying consciousness.

We are unwittingly taking actions based on our preferences and repulsions, our beliefs and ideas. When we become aware of them, we notice that what we hear is not necessarily true. When someone says something negative, we react. We usually have little control over this reaction. We do not have choice. Becoming aware of this is the beginning of our reclaiming the innate authority that the soul actually has over the papier-mâché world—the world of the mind and vital and body. We are beginning to recover our ability to choose to live life free of their influence, by this act of restraining these things, regulating them, not believing what they tell us, and not being sucked into the habit of our reactive patterns, desires, and cravings. We begin to withdraw our consent to go there.

When we make that effort, we begin to bring who we truly are into that particular part of ourselves. Without this intelligent effort and self-control, the papier-mâché rules. Your ability to go forward is limited, because the papier-mâché person just keeps adding layers so it can be more solid and real and important, so it can protect itself from being diminished or broken, so it doesn't have to feel the emptiness within. It will keep accumulating more and more layers of karma to try to preserve its apparent reality, even though in the middle it is empty. It is through sacrifice that we withdraw our consent to continue the papier-mâché-ing.

Building a papier-mâché world is not evil. Evil is actually just error. It is that which takes us away from the truth of ourselves. Good is that which takes us toward it. Therefore, feeding these inclinations that keep our identity associated with our papier-mâché self could be seen as an unconscious error, while withdrawing from taking these actions is good. This is a way to understand sacrifice.

Material, Vital, and Mental Sacrifices

190. *Some perform sacrifice with material possessions, some offer austerity as sacrifice, others follow any path of yoga as sacrifice, while some earnest seekers perform sacrifice in the form of wisdom through the study of scriptures.*
191. *Some offer the vital air as sacrifice by controlling breathing, offering inhalation into exhalation or exhalation into inhalation.*
192. *Others offer the life-breath by controlling their diet. All these are different types of sacrifices offered by seekers to destroy evil.*

There are different types of sacrifices, such as material sacrifices, vital sacrifices, and mental sacrifices. In the Vedic tradition there are many food and flower offerings, which are material sacrifices. For us it might be donating money or giving of your time to charity. Or a material sacrifice might be simplifying our material life or getting rid of unnecessary baggage. With fewer material possessions, there is less demand and less requirement to play in this papier-mâché world. We pull back from those things that we had previously made important, like our house, our car, and other material possessions. Material sacrifice is the first form of sacrifice. It has a certain beneficial power, because in material simplicity we are less distracted, less obligated. We can begin to pull away from all the energy and demands that possessions require and look at what is essential, what is true.

The second type of sacrifice is self-control of the vital—our emotions, reactivity, and drives. Instead of letting moods run us one way or another, we consciously restrain the actions these prompt in us. We then can see that we have been allowing ourselves to get caught in the frenetic environment of ordinary life.

"Some offer the vital air as sacrifice by controlling breathing, offering inhalation into exhalation or exhalation into inhalation." Here the Gita is pointing to the use of conscious breathing to control emotional reactions. One example is to count to ten before you act. You learn control when you don't let the emotions that arise overtake you. If something causes a reaction in you, just count to ten and then you have some self-control. Breath is a very powerful tool for pulling back from impulses or inclinations. In many spiritual practices breath control, or pranayama, is a powerful means to gain control over the vital impulsive nature.

We bring forward our innate intelligence when we pull back from those things we previously made important. We see how these things bound us to our papier-mâché self. The strength that comes with this gives us the ability to choose differently, to discover a new way to be in our life. This opens the door to that inner peace which comes in time. In time these things happen spontaneously; we speed up the process by letting go of our old ways of being.

Another sacrifice is to control our eating. I have observed that controlling the diet can bring about significant change.

Real shifts can occur. It is as if we reclaim the power over our lives. Instead of eating impulsively, you start choosing what you eat and apply more intelligence over that part of yourself. It empowers us; we become more alive and interested when we are able to do so. I have seen people make huge strides when they are no longer as strongly anchored to their impulsive eating habits.

Harnessing the Fire of Knowledge

193. *Yogis who enjoy the benefits of this world after performing sacrifices attain to the eternal state, but one who does not perform any sacrifice cannot gain happiness in this world nor in any of the other worlds.*
194. *The Vedas talk of many such sacrifices but all these are born of action. When you will know the truth behind these sacrifices you will be free from the bondage of action.*

In other words, if you are performing a sacrifice for personal gain, such as controlling your diet so you can look good, then that sacrifice is not a pure sacrifice. It is another back-door way of enhancing the papier-mâché self. It is another way of keeping us entrenched in our egoic identity, although a seemingly better version of ourselves than before. The initial sacrifice may have been true, but then the ego takes credit for it. Or just as likely the ego converts a true pure sacrifice into an expectation, or disappointment, or resentment.

The ego tries to lay claim on the spiritual path all the time. It likes to claim how awakened it is or how good it is and how noble it is. It just makes a new, improved version of ego, another papier-mâché edition, the spiritual papier-mâché edition. Look, it has wings. It looks lighter even though it is just another way of becoming more solid. This is not sacrifice. In fact, the sacrifice loses its value and the progress is lost. The status quo is maintained. You are veiled from the soul in a new way. You are veiled from the truth of who you are in a new way. The patterns of the old ego are reinforced. It's a catch-22. Unless you are connected to your higher Self, you cannot perform sacrifices perfectly, and yet you can't get there without performing sacrifices. You can't win for losing.

This is the paradox. You take action with no certainty that it will produce a result. This is what Gita is trying to show us: We have to sacrifice the sacrifice itself. You have to detach yourself from the effort. You detach yourself from experiencing any spiritual benefit. You are doing your spiritual practices day in and day out, and nothing is happening. That is perfect as long as you can accept "nothing happening." You are, in fact, undoing the ego's need for something to happen. Nothing happening is closer to the truth of you than something happening. Papier-mâché loves something happening—more papier-mâché. It means I'm real, I'm here, and I exist. I'm upset and struggling. The papier-mâché person loves that. It does not know how to be with "nothing happening," with emptiness.

The consequences of life keep us bumping into things. Chunks of our papier-mâché get knocked off. But immediately we are programmed to patch it back up. We create a strategy to recover what we were. But what are we recovering? We are recovering our papier-mâché self. We are going back to cutting newspaper strips and pasting more layers to it. It keeps us busy, believing this is the right thing to do to keep our world together. Yet all that is needed to wipe it all out is a strong wind, an accident, or the death of a loved one. It is a false sense of self; it is temporary and unstable.

More important than the action is the attitude or intent we have about the action. If the intent of the action is to undo, to diminish the ego, to diminish the way we have assumed we are, on any plane—materially, vitally, relationally, and mentally—then we are effective in diminishing the habit of our separate identity. With this kind of intention, every failure, loss, defeat, or vulnerability is progress. We are beginning to move into that which we never wanted to experience. The function of a papier-mâché identity is that it allows us to deny or avoid all kinds of unwanted experiences. Each layer of papier-mâché is an avoidance strategy that hides what we have avoided experiencing or knowing in the course of our life. As long as these layers remain, we remain bound, limited by these unmet, unwanted insights or experiences.

No ego would consciously try to unravel itself. The ego never seeks its own undoing. It is only your true self—that which is the source of you—that seeks to undo this false self, this false premise of who you are and what the world is. The Gita says:

195. *Sacrifice through knowledge is superior to sacrifice performed through material objects because all actions invariably culminate in knowledge.*

Any action taken in the state of knowledge undoes the ego. Any action taken from this enhanced state of knowledge is extremely effective in undoing our false self, and its previous habits.

The third chapter of the Gita says, *"Senses are said to be more powerful than the body, but greater than the senses is the mind, superior to the mind is the intellect, and superior to the intellect is the Self."* Material sacrifices that are associated with the body and senses have a certain power. Vital sacrifices associated with the drives and emotions have greater power. Sacrifices of the mental, the beliefs and habits of thinking, have still greater power. And sacrifices of the intellect, the need to rationalize, justify, and protect the constructs of the mental existence, have even more power. But a greater power still is the true Self. That is the knowledge being talked about. We can call it the psychic being. We can call that the "what," the part of us that has thoughts, but isn't the thoughts. Has feelings but isn't the feelings. Has sensations, has a body, but isn't those things. This is the "what" able to separate itself from the "who."

So when you reside in the psychic being, when you are in connection to the radiance of the Sat, which is what the psychic being is—the interface between the soul and the personality—something of truth is revealed to the personality. From that place a fire is brought forward that undoes the inclinations to perpetuate the old karmas, the old habits of action and reaction. An action taken from this place carries with it tremendous effectiveness in tearing down and dismantling this papier-mâché construct. It is a spontaneous action that is performed without any conscious knowledge that a sacrifice is involved. It happens spontaneously, without apparent effort. The divine takes over the effort, the sacrifice is being done automatically.

This process, once it starts, is purposeful. It moves you toward something, not away from something. So when this sacrifice of knowledge comes, you are no longer looking at your papier-mâché life. You are turning your attention to that which is the source of our attention, what it is you are heading toward, and in the process it automatically dismantles your papier-mâché life. That action is done spontaneously out of aspiration and longing for that which is coming, not out of ambition or discipline or control. Yet all your previous sacrifices prepared you for this. Sacrifices at the level of the material, the mental, relationships, beliefs, or the vital drives is what prepares you to come to this state of actionless-action. The quality of knowledge this type of action brings is a fire that burns all types of karma.

And now there is spontaneous combustion. Suddenly the log that was rolled up against the fire and smoldering, ignites and burns. Burning consumes more and more and grows in intensity the more it burns. This is when one crosses the threshold. It is like sending a rocket into outer space. At first you send the rocket up, but if it doesn't have enough strength, it comes crashing back down, and you fall back to how it was before. Later you try again; and even though there is more effort and you are really determined, it still comes crashing back down again, back to the same old, same old. After a while it seems that as much as we change, the more we remain the same. This is how it was for me the first fifty years of my life. The more I strived to make things better, the more it seemed I came back to the same crappy old place I was in before.

But when the force that awakened me came, it pushed me into my own orbit. I broke free of the pull of the gravity of my old life. I never came back to my old life. Such an event happens when, through conscious or unconscious sacrifices, we gather sufficient momentum to exceed the pull of the gravity of our old life and enter into a new way of being, into our own orbit. At first it might be wavering or on the edge of falling, but if we remain steady in our practices, we stabilize in a new state of being—beyond the pull of the world. That is what this chapter is pointing to. The fire of knowledge is what gets us to that place.

Three Ways to Benefit from an Enlightened Master

196. *Know this knowledge from the enlightened masters. They are the knowers of Truth. Gain this knowledge from them through humility, inquiry, and by rendering service to them.*

Here's the joker in the deck. Here's the get-out-of-jail-free card—the enlightened master. This is what Krishna is revealing here. What is described in this chapter is very difficult to attain on your own. It is very, very tough to get sufficient momentum to get into orbit. There are many efforts made and many failures. There is no assurance. But what often happens is that when we are almost able to make it with our own effort, a being shows up in our life who is able to augment our capacity to go further, to be connected to that fire. They bring the fire in themselves, which is already fully animated, and transmit it to you. Your own longing, your own need to reach this state, is thereby strengthened. You find yourself able to come to a sustainable relationship with the truth of yourself.

This is the role of the enlightened master. What is an enlightened master? An enlightened master may have a papier-mâché body, but they are not their papier-mâché body. They may have a personality and limitations. But in fact they are now the universal being. They are the air surrounding the air within your papier-mâché self. They hold this space for you so that you may find that same thing in yourself. Creation was designed to bring these enlightened beings to help you go where you couldn't so that you can complete the journey.

There are three ways to benefit from an enlightened master. First is through humility. Humility is receptivity. Come with receptivity, appreciation, openness—not with arrogance, demand, expectation, or complaint. Come with an empty cup, not a full cup. The more empty the cup, the more you will get. It is through the thinning of the papier-mâché self that we make ourselves ready. Combustion is then more likely to occur.

The second way is self-inquiry. I call this taking personal responsibility for your own issues, the ability to look inwardly at what is going on in you. It is the ability to see why the world is showing up the way it is for you, as an opportunity for you to meet what is hidden or obscured, instead of trying to fix or get rid of. You begin to see what in you is being pulled or pushed. Without inquiry and personal responsibility, you are run by factors outside of yourself. In addition you can use the enlightened being as the opportunity to surrender your ego, to undo your point of view, rather than to continue to reinforce your existing ego. It is not about getting anything outwardly. The value is inward. It may look as if nothing is happening. It may look awful at times. Your job in self-inquiry is to recognize the failure of your old ways, the failure of running away. Wherever you go, there you are—the false self. It is just waiting to come back, to show up again, in another form, with another teacher, relationship, circumstance, or job. Now you must develop the capacity to stay put, to stay in the fire, to stay with the process.

The third way is service to the enlightened master. Service is self-giving without any benefit for yourself. It could be for the enlightened master or their mission. The more you serve their work, the more you benefit spiritually. An enlightened being is always burning. He is automatically in continuous sacrifice. But he has no need for any of the benefit of sacrifice. He is already empty. So the benefit goes to those who turn to him and are assisting in the sacrifice. Outwardly the benefit may not be apparent. It may look like a lot of work. But when you are in service with a spiritual master, your sacrifice has tremendous effectiveness in burning your remaining karmas. You are hanging onto a rocket that is taking you into orbit. This is the power of one's relationship to the enlightened master. You can go as far as you can hang on.

These three—humility, self-inquiry, and service—are very powerful tools to further ignite that which is burning within already. A piece of the sun is ignited in you. And all it wants to do is merge with the sun that is everywhere. It is just looking for a way to get back home. Your papier-mâché construct will be consumed from the inside out until it is just a thin sheet. When paste gets hot enough, it becomes a transparent shell.

For an enlightened master the fire within has burned the papier-mâché—but there is still this transparent shell that somehow remains intact despite the intense pressure and heat. That thin transparent membrane is what knows its own enlightenment. It is what knows that it is merging with the sun. It is the drop, aware that it has now merged with the ocean. It is the remnant of the old self, the papier-mâché puppet, hollowed out, empty, and free. A person is still there, talking, walking, acting, and doing things, but it is very superficial. Within, they are a vast infinity. This vast emptiness within is what makes one an enlightened master.

STAYING IN THE FIRE

200. *Here in this world there is nothing more powerful to purify the consciousness than knowledge. This knowledge is realized automatically in the course of time when one pursues this path of yoga sincerely.*
201. *This knowledge can be acquired by one who has faith and devotion, follows self-control and pursues the path of yoga diligently. When one realizes this knowledge one immediately attains supreme peace.*

This is the greatest assurance of the Bhagavad Gita. "*This knowledge is realized automatically in the course of time when one pursues this path of yoga sincerely.*" It takes time, guys. It takes time. This papier-mâché construct is not just of your own making. It has been made from thousands and thousands of years of matter developing and evolving, becoming more and more sophisticated and complex in the process, until the human form was created. The debris of this process is inherited through our ancestors, plus whatever we add to it this lifetime. So it takes time to be undone. This process of persevering in the process, staying on track, even when there is no hope or evidence that we are getting there, is the key.

That which is looking for evidence is the part of yourself that is being undone. It has no way of registering evidence, in its papier-mâché mind, of the truth of itself. Papier-mâché minds can only keep track of papier-mâché things. So when you are in a state of truth, there is nowhere for this evidence to be stored, to be remembered. It is of a completely different order of being than your papier-mâché existence. Persistent effort, without attachment to any outcome even when there is no evidence or even when there is contrary evidence, is the secret to full transformation, full realization.

202. *One who lacks the capacity of discrimination, is devoid of faith, and is assailed by doubts is destined to be doomed in this path. For the doubting soul there is no hope nor happiness in this world nor in the world beyond.*

203. *Arjuna, actions do not bind him who has renounced action through yoga, whose doubts are destroyed by knowledge and who is established in the Self.*

It may be very difficult to stay in the fire in this stage of the journey. The smoke and the ash of your own destruction may even veil you from knowing that it is your ego that is afire. The secret here is not to say, "This doesn't work for me" or "I can do it elsewhere." You must realize the futility of fleeing. It requires faith to stay with the process and not run off to try to recover something of your past, or to avoid something that is rising up that you have avoided all your life, or many lives. Faith is not trust. Faith is not belief. Trust is in the vital plane. Belief is in the mental plane. Faith comes from the innermost being. Faith comes from the soul.

204. *Therefore, cut with your sword of knowledge this doubt that is caused by ignorance that abides in your heart. Follow the path of yoga. Stand up and fight.*

Faith keeps us on the trajectory track. Without faith you cannot endure this process. Doubt is your enemy. "This is not working. This is not for me. This is the wrong teacher. This is the wrong group." The ego will come up with ferocity. It will seek to destroy all progress. Although it may not be very apparent, the ego, through doubt, will seek to undo the progress you have made to date. So cut doubt with the sword of knowledge. Cut it with the fire of your own aspiration, by aligning with the truth of what you are heading toward.

Yet it is hard to know what you are heading toward at this stage of the journey. You have knowledge but it is not ultimate knowledge. It is a new kind of knowing, a different kind of knowing. Your actions that are aligned with truth are not yet embedded, not yet sufficiently integrated or part of your whole person.

In this fourth chapter you are still struggling to make the spiritual life real, to make this pursuit real to your papier-mâché self. You are still vulnerable. This leads to the entry point of the fifth chapter, the Yoga of Renunciation, the next stage of this process.

The Yoga of Renunciation of Action

One who has realized the Brahman lives eternally in identity
with Brahman and does not feel perturbed when he comes
across unpleasant situations nor does he feel elated when
he receives something pleasant. His intellect is firm
and he is free from delusion.
⟶ VERSE 224

Having come out of dejection, applied our discrimination, taken action to bring us out of suffering, and learned the knowledge and sacrifices that break us out of our habitual egoic nature, we are ready to embark on The Yoga of Renunciation. We can now begin to align our outer lives with our inner consciousness to further expand our ability to know the truth of what we are.

THE EFFORTFUL PART OF THE JOURNEY

The knowledge that comes in Chapter 4 is knowledge of the truth of ourselves. But it is coming through layers of ego. Maybe through the transparency of our heart we feel a connection to something greater than ourselves. Or maybe through the greater awareness of our intelligence or the more limited mental capacities of the mind we sense something greater than ourselves. All of these may be more open, but they are still fragile and uncertain. You could still fall and collapse during this stage of the journey. You could have a setback. Anger, fear, or rage could arise and overtake you. Or you could have an accident, or lose a loved one, or a job. You could be thrown back down into dejection and need to climb your way back up to this threshold. You gather more strength by repeatedly going through this process of the first four chapters, from dejection to discrimination to action to gathering knowledge.

These first five chapters of the Gita define the most effortful part of the journey. We have to work and apply effort continuously to bring forward a new consciousness and to overcome the inertia, the habits of our old lives, not to retreat back into what we were used to. The inclination is to return to that which was comfortable and familiar. Now in this chapter there is a greater capacity to spontaneously apply effort to bring this new quality of being into our personality and life. We are more able to step back from our old self and thereby are more able to restrain the old tendencies. The more effort we apply, the greater our strength to do so. But at this stage it is still not strong enough. We must still struggle against the pull of lower tendencies. This is where we are at the beginning of Chapter 5.

RENUNCIATION—A DIRTY WORD

Renunciation is a dirty word in the West. It sounds like the opposite of what we want. We think we want happiness and enjoyment, comfort and abundance—not renunciation. A lot of people fall away in this part of the journey. They are not quite ready. The pull to the familiar is still too enticing. It is not clear that where you are headed is going to be worth it. Do you recognize this in yourself?

Chapter 5 introduces us to the point of no return, a point where the momentum toward God or Truth is sufficient to break out of the gravitational pull of the ego. This transition, this shift in consciousness, seems like a small thing when it occurs. There's no great fanfare. It is just a little shift, a little twist, and suddenly the world we have known before loses its importance. It loses its reality. In fact this is an inexplicable shift, an inexplicable change. It occurs when the consciousness has gathered sufficient momentum to break the pull of the world and turns to the world of spirit. It goes into its own orbit. Sustained effort is more natural than the inclination to return back to the old ways. Like a teeter-totter, the point of no return is now weighted in favor of the spirit versus matter. This shift, when it comes, still needs to be integrated, to be established. Time and effort are needed to come out of the world of error, samskara, and karma. The outer life needs to align with the inner.

KNOWLEDGE VERSUS ACTION

Chapter 5, The Yoga of Renunciation of Action (Karma-Sannyasa Yoga), begins with Arjuna asking what is the difference between the path of knowledge (renunciation) and action:

The Blessed Lord said:

206. *Both the paths, renunciation and action, lead one to liberation. Of the two, however, the path of action is superior to renunciation of action . . ."*
208. *The ignorant say that the path of knowledge and the path of action lead to divergent results, but not the wise. If someone follows sincerely either of these paths, he gets the fruits of both.*

Arjuna is confused about whether the path of knowledge or the path of action is best. Both are important, Krishna says. The goal attained by one is equal to the goal attained by the other. More than that, each is necessary for the fulfillment of the other.

Without knowledge of the soul, action will be tainted by desire and attachment. But without action, without sacrifice, one is likely to end up a hypocrite. Parts of their life may know the truth and other parts may not. These seekers tend to be *pragnyavadis*—hypocrites—those who preach about how to live but are not living it themselves.

Without action, knowledge is incomplete. You haven't tested and integrated it. You may be ascending in knowledge, in your awareness of spirit, but you are still overtaken or challenged by your old life. Yoga requires continuous and conscious effort, often over long periods of time, to become established in ourselves. We have to apply what we know into our lives to make it real. Both knowledge and action, together, are necessary for this to happen.

Just to be clear, the kind of knowledge pointed to in the Gita is of a different order than mere learning or understanding. We in the West tend to value learned mental knowledge, information we have gathered, read, seen, or heard. There is a kind of satisfaction to read a book about the nature of the soul, or the nature of consciousness, or the nature of our bondage. But that in itself doesn't change anything. Action is the test, the key to create real change. On the other hand it is also true that without true knowledge, the action is likely to be ineffective. Without discrimination that comes from connecting to spirit, the action is not likely to be focused or effective. It will go this way or that way.

When we speak of action detached from outcome, we are really talking about all outcomes. One who lives in a state of renunciation has let go of all attachment, detached from all outcomes. This is what it means to be a true renunciate, a sannyasi. You can't get there with just the mind. Understanding will only prepare you. You have to have a connection to spirit, the truth of your soul. Otherwise the action will end up serving the desires and inclinations of the old nature. One will veer off course. You can fool yourself into thinking you are detached if things are going the way you want them. But when they are not, you realize that wasn't the case. This tests the truth of your knowledge and can expand your relationship with your inner reality.

The integration of knowledge and action is being brought together at this stage due to the effort, sacrifice and sense control described in Chapter 4. Eventually knowledge, with action, starts undoing that which has us addicted to action that binds us. The strength of our yogic action takes us into a new relationship to our own existence based on the greatest light that we have at any one moment. Krishna confirms:

210. *Renunciation is difficult without performing action. When one follows the path of action by keeping his mind fixed on God he will quickly attain Brahman.*

Turning your attention away from the things of the world and turning your attention on spirit exclusively is the secret, focusing on where you are headed, rather than where you have been. Turning away from the world—as either something we have to control or as our source of satisfaction—to where we are headed is a very important transition in consciousness.

FOUR INDICATORS OF ALIGNMENT

211. *One whose mind is fixed on God and who has mastered self-control, whose heart is pure and who has identified himself with the Self in all, remains untainted even while performing action.*

This verse gives us four indicators on how to orient our consciousness. The first is to have our attention fixed on God. We have to have a strong aspiration for spirit or a deep longing for God, either in our awareness, our intelligence, or in the pull of our heart.

Second is to have sufficient control over our impulses and inclinations, the samskaras and karmas, so as to not be run this way or that way by them.

The third indicator, a pure heart, is to have a sincere turning toward Truth and God. Sincerity is not possible unless you have had enough contact with the inner reality you are, your soul. Without that, your sincerity will be weak. It will be determined by your mood or your sattwa cycle. Once it gets difficult, often conflict arises and our sincerity collapses. Then you are an instrument of your preferences, attractions, and repulsions, rejecting or manipulating your environment so you can have it your way again. You create a story for yourself so as to justify why you are returning to where you have been. You have to keep the connection to your purpose spiritually, to where you are headed in order for sincerity to be integral enough, to have sufficient strength, to take you beyond what you have not yet renounced.

This fourth indicator, "*Who has identified himself with the Self in all,*" is the ability to experience the divine in one's self and to the same divine in others, and is the most difficult one. Our identification with ourselves as a personality, with our thoughts, opinions, and beliefs as real, with our moods and feelings as real, is the crux of the problem. We have become identified with the vehicle that we are occupying, and all its aspects: sensations, emotions, drives, wants, and mental stories. We have been overtaken. We have lost touch with "what" we really are and are lost in the "who" we are. We have become absorbed in this personality that we think we are and its attachments or wants. Everything becomes personal; we take everything personally based on how the world shows up for us. What is good, bad, scary, interesting—are all shaped through the lens of our old self.

This identification with the content of our body and personality is where we have lost ourselves. The error is in the identification, losing ourself in what we associate with. This is the habit of ego. Prior to the end of this journey the error is almost complete, even on the spiritual path. "Who is gaining the knowledge?" "Well, I am gaining the knowledge." "Who is gaining the experience?" "Well, I am gaining the experience. I am a good yogi today. I am a bad yogi today." This is identification.

Identification with our personal ego in relationship with truth is the crux of the problem. How can we step out of this? Even thinking about something different from our identification is another form of ego. It's a very tricky and difficult thing.

Experiencing the divine in yourself and others indicates you have come to this point of renunciation. The spiritual energy is saturating your system and the sense of individual self is not able to dominate you as it did before. You have discovered you are the "what," the witness or the context for the "who," the content of your previous life. Any number of things can be happening at this transition. You can have a wonderful sense of freedom and expansion of consciousness, or you can become anxious and unstable, or both.

At this point the conditioning of ego is to try to reestablish itself or find some kind of new stability. So when you step out of your old self, you often become vulnerable, confused, fearful, angry, etc. You feel very unstable. Your life feels like it has fallen apart. Your old self's beliefs, opinions, habits, and routines seem false. You don't sleep well. The food doesn't taste good. Sex has lost its appeal. You are not as interested in friends or movies or books. This is the beginning of true renunciation.

It's a difficult transition. But it is a pivotal movement away from bondage toward truth. I see this again and again. The human ego keeps trying to return to what is familiar. When I see someone who is working with me who is very happy and content with his or her yoga, I frown. When I see someone edgy and miserable and complaining, I smile, because I know that what is going on is a true shift from identification with the limited self to identification with the true Self.

In Unity With One's Ego

212. *One who is steadfast in yoga always feels, "I am not doing anything." Such a knower of truth feels that all these actions like seeing, hearing, touching, smelling, eating, walking, sleeping, breathing.*
213. *Talking, excreting, grasping, opening and shutting the eyes, etc., are being done by the senses for the object of pleasure.*
214. *When someone is capable of performing actions fully linked with God he acquires no sin, as a lotus leaf does not get wet although submerged in water.*

The problem is that we are so linked to what we are identified with. It is "me" who wants dinner, it is "me" who wants comfort, and it is "me" who has behaved poorly or nobly. This "me" "me" "me" is identification, and it is what keeps us bound to the habit of the separate self. Every time you are vested in an action, either consciously or unconsciously, you are feeding that inclination, that desire, that fear. Choosing not to be with one person but choosing to be with someone else is feeding the mechanism of repulsion or attraction. Even if we are doing it unconsciously, it is binding. It is continuing the pattern of karma that keeps us identified with our separate existence.

Eventually you come to a place in consciousness where it is not you acting, but these things are just arising. You are not identified with them. You are the space in which these things are arising. You are the context for the content of you. This state of freedom comes when one has broken out of the identification with oneself as a separate person. This state took a long time to come to me. I was long on the journey—for many years—before I realized that it was just the machine acting, not me acting. I was in the habit of constantly judging and evaluating myself, comparing myself with others. I believed the thought that those feelings were mine. So it took me a long time to break out of this habit—especially in the mental plane—of constantly evaluating if it was going well or not. Of course there was a growing acceptance and tolerance, but the real shift took a long time to happen.

These verses are pointing to something that is quite rare unless one has made a sudden, abrupt shift, and even then it takes time for that point of view to establish itself, to become integrated, to come to the point of no return. It is a completely different relationship with existence. Up until that point we are still accumulating karma. We are still feeding the existing structure of karma, even if we are unraveling it in moments of our connection to God or moments of unity with the vast awareness of the all-pervading Reality. Those are the two kinds of oneness—merger or unity—that come on the journey. Merger is in the heart; unity is in the awareness. They are two aspects of the same thing. Ultimately completion in one aspect leads to completion in the other. They complete each other.

Until that has come, you are in unity with your ego. You are in unity with your motivations. You have merged with your desires. You have merged with your wants and needs. You have merged with your story. This mechanism of identification is the key characteristic of consciousness until it discovers its true nature. It keeps identifying and trying to make something that is separate from itself to be part of itself. It aggregates, it adds to itself. "This is the person I love. I want them in my house. I want them in my bed." You are trying to make something that is separate become part of you, like eating food. It is an aggregation that gives the ego a false sense of security and stability. It is a relatively more stable condition than without those things.

For me this state of unity came spontaneously soon after my awakening. I realized that nothing else mattered, and I closed down my outer life and left to live in India for six years as a celibate, having little to do with my past. But in time I was able to reenter the parts of my old life that were aligned with my new consciousness. I was able to integrate those parts into my newly unfolding life.

This is the habit of ego: to acquire more ego, more stability, more reality, because it knows it can never be truly stable. It can only get to a place where the instability is not so apparent. This relative happiness comes and goes, it is dependent on one of those things we have acquired from the external world to help our ego feel stable. This includes the experiences and knowledge acquired on the spiritual path. We try figuring out how things work; we acquire some knowledge, so our mind gets a little more stable as we feel we understand. That quiets the mental, but its identity is still based on instability, not on stability. It is trying to mask the inherent instability of mind, body, and emotions. Consciousness is always unstable and restless, seeking to become stable. The true state of stability comes when we are identified with that which is eternally silent and still: the Self within, absolutely stable with no need for anything else but itself. That is when consciousness knows itself fully.

The Great Paradox

215. *Yogis perform action with senses, mind, intellect, and body only for self-purification, shaking off all attachment.*

A true yogi has the capacity to perform actions only for self-purification. I tell those around me to get a job, work hard, put in full effort, and not to expect any outcome. I call it learning to work for free, with nothing in it for yourself. You do your yoga, your meditation, your spiritual practice, you attend talks, you practice self-inquiry, and you also detach from the outcome. The ego says, "Wait a second. I've been with you for a year or more and nothing is happening. Where's my payoff? How come I don't have more experiences?" That is the continuous complaint of ego, even when spiritual progress has been happening, even when experiences and revelations have occurred.

Ego only tracks what serves ego; it forgets everything else. The restlessness of desire wants to see evidence, yet as long as our ego is looking for some proof, be it from human action or spiritual action, we start to doubt, question, and fall into the trap of ego, which wants us to return to the old life. As long as there is attachment to outcome, the spiritual path is going to be very difficult. We have to put both feet on the path; we have to sincerely commit—then doubt grows quiet.

216. *Having abandoned the fruits of action, a yogi attains permanent peace, but due to his attachment for the fruit, the undisciplined one is bound by his own actions prompted by his desires.*

Abandoning the fruits of action sounds like madness. Without a profitable outcome, why do anything? Why bother to make all the effort? Here is the paradox: Without action, nothing can change; yet being attached to the outcome of action also keeps you stuck in the same old paradigm, inevitably becoming dissatisfied. Actually, yoga is an effective way to become stable, but you will remain unstable because the ego is laying claim to the outcome of your yoga.

Abandoning the fruits of action means you have to actively reject a preferred outcome, the fruit. Doing the action as an offering means you offer it up; you don't take it back later or take credit for it. That's not an offering; that's a calculation. An offering is selfless giving. It does it for free. You give it to the divine. You have to keep relinquishing the ego's desire to lay claim to the effort. For example, "Now I am a yogi. Now I am living with a spiritual teacher. Now I am doing all this spiritual practice. See how good and special I am." That's the ego. Or it goes to the other side: "I am wasting my time. Nothing is happening here. These people are all pains. Why should I continue?"

The ego lays claim to everything. Only by consciously abandoning this mechanism in yourself will you keep on track. You need to realize that this is not about getting something that you imagine is outside of yourself—be it an idea, a feeling, or an attainment—but it is about losing everything. It is about undoing, not redoing. It is not about creating a better ego or a better kind of happiness.

Yet here is a crazy paradox. If you can grasp this paradox, you can begin to understand the nature of your sacrifice. Even though actions will be ineffective to some degree because you are invested in the outcome, they are not useless. If you don't make effort, even if it comes from ego, it will never be possible to move into a state where there is no effort or where you are not laying claim to the outcome, actionless-action. Tricky stuff. This is the key, though.

217. *Renouncing all the action urges of the mind and happily dwelling as the ruler in the city of nine gates, the self-disciplined yogi neither acts nor makes others act.*

There are two parts to this. First, it points to a state of mastery, to not let the world overtake you, to not get caught up in your reactions or beliefs or preferences or repulsions by controlling what comes in through the senses and the openings in the body, the nine gates: two ears, two eyes, two nostrils, a mouth, urinary opening and anus. This is the mastery that comes with renunciation.

When you get to that place of mastery, what are you ruling? You, the central self, the part of your ego that is aligned with the inner Self, has come forward as the dominant authority over the personality and body that you inhabit, rather than all the impulses, inclinations, and desires that come with these. The human being is a transitional being between the animal and the divine. It is not just an animal driven by instincts and impulses; nor is it yet aware of its inherent divine reality. In this transitional zone we are constantly being pulled downward by our animal nature, even while we are being pulled upward by our ideals and inspirations. Once we come to the point of mastery of the downward pull, then the movement upward automatically strengthens and gains momentum.

The key is where you put your attention. If you put your attention into what binds you, then you reinforce your bondage. If you put your attention into what frees you, then you will move toward freedom, automatically undoing the pull of the lower nature, of the ego. When you are the ruler of the city with nine gates, then your restraint over your senses allows you to avoid acting out old karmas or creating new karmas. When you come to the state of truth, others can say positive or critical things about you and you don't react.

One who is in that state is undoing the hold of the world and is moving toward greater truth and consciousness. One measure of this state is when spoken to frankly or directly of things you usually would not want to hear, you don't get upset or defensive, but instead feel empowered. Then you can know your higher Self is at play. When action arises from this place it creates no karma, no consequences. Then one is in the state of actionless-action. This is one of the indicators. The divinity within is acting. When the divinity acts, whatever action it takes is transformative, is bringing forward greater truth and wisdom.

218. *God neither determines the doership nor the deeds of men nor the union of action with its fruit. These are all done by prakriti.*
219. *God never receives the virtue nor the sin of anyone. As knowledge is enveloped by ignorance, people become victims of delusion.*
220. *But for those whose ignorance of the Self is destroyed by the knowledge of the Self, the wisdom in them shines like the sun and reveals the Supreme.*

God neither determines the virtue nor the sin of anyone; we do that. We do that to ourselves through our unwitting identification with the vehicle. When we do something "bad," it is the human in us judging. If we were animals there would be no self-judgment, no good or bad, no right or wrong. Only humans judge, evaluate, and create a watchful overlord: We're going to hell or we're going to heaven. Yet if society had not created structures like this through law, religion, or superstition, we would still be animals, just trying to eat each other or avoid being eaten.

This is a stage of consciousness where the lower nature had to be managed for mankind to evolve. We had to create a judgmental principle in order to organize our human existence so that evolution, rather than devolution, could occur. When we beat ourselves up or think we have done something really wrong, it is not a sin, it is an error. And when we think we are so great and smart and have done something right, it is also an error. They are both errors, as if there is some authority watching over us and we are judging ourselves from that authority. When we beat ourselves up unnecessarily, we also reinforce a negative pattern of judgment in us that keeps us small, powerless, and stupid. We think we are those things but we are not. We are the consciousness that inhabits a vehicle that carries both positive and negative inclinations, for good or ill.

If you are aware that your vehicle is just a machine, like a car, and you are in the car being taken on a ride, then your identification isn't that you are doing it, but that the car is doing it. Thinking that you are the one who is making the error or right action is all part of the identification with the vehicle. We don't want to throw out morality or right or wrong actions, because it is an effective interim organizing principle. But the Gita is pointing to the state where you go beyond right or wrong. When you are in that state you are no longer pulled by the forces that create error; there is no sin or virtue. You are pulled to your divinity. The story about us being a good person or bad gets unraveled. We are neither. We can be either only from the point of view of mind, of our own judgment.

There is another part to this. There are actions that work and actions that don't work; actions that are effective in taking you to oneness and truth and actions that are not effective in taking you to oneness and truth. Sin is nothing but error. It is just missing the target. Virtue is nothing but hitting the target, being appropriate to the situation that is arising. It is not about heaven or hell, or good or bad. So look at what works and what doesn't work relative to your purpose. After a while you become effective by choosing what works. Judgment of yourself or others is an error. The part of you that judges yourself or another is just ego judging ego.

There is no God in heaven that judges you. There is nothing but your own guilt and shame, your own inherited judge that does that. When you live aligned with your highest light that follows the promptings of your higher Self, then life starts to look good or virtuous. For you it is just heading toward the light. It is just going with what is aligned with your purpose, with what works. And once you find out what works, you just want more of that. Once you get hip to what doesn't work, you stop doing it. When you do what works and come into relationship with your true nature, then there is happiness, a feeling of connection—a radiance. It comes from connecting to your inner source. That which you are is sufficient to come through all the layers of your ego personality, bringing peace, calmness, and stability to your environment.

The Point of No Return

221. *One whose mind and intellect are constantly absorbed in the Supreme, who considers Him to be the highest, whose sins have been washed away by wisdom, reaches a state of no return.*

This is the point of no return. It is a tremendous gift. It's when you step out of the box. You step out of "you." It's an indescribable shift. When it comes, you can't fit back into the box again. It's a waking up to the illusion of the sandbox you have been playing in all your life. It's stepping out of your habits such that you can't go back into them for very long. When this shift in consciousness happens, at least some part of you—for some it is in the heart and for some it is in the mind—steps out of your identification with yourself as a separate ego. You become that indescribable quality of being that is outside of that paradigm.

Once this happens—and it can be slow or fast—it takes a long time to fully understand what has happened. When it happens you can no longer go back and become a human being. You try. You go back and try to make money and have relationships, but it all feels empty. You try to get pleasure from the things that used to give you pleasure, but they no longer are pleasurable. This is the irrevocable moment for any soul's journey. The key is the shift in identity from the "who" you are to the "what" you are, from untruth to truth.

To come to the point of no return does not necessarily mean you are free or liberated yet. But it is a crucial transition, the beginning of the next stage of the journey, where the effort to progress is no longer as effortful. At this stage the consciousness is no longer pulled into its old egoic identity. It is becoming more absorbed in the truth of itself; it is now possible to turn to that which is greater, truer than you've been able to be before.

This shift may start as an experience of separation from your old life, a loss of interest, a dispassion. You notice detachment and calm where before you were fearful or anxious. You are no longer as reactive; you notice a quieting in your system and a pull to meditation and spiritual things. You no longer have a pull to be with friends or family or to respond to them. There is more spontaneous detachment and letting go. There is still the habit in play that keeps your attention on the old life and the world, but it is no longer gripping you as it had prior to this shift, to this point of no return.

THE SYMPTOMS OF THE SHIFT

222. *A truly wise man sees the same soul present in the form of a learned person, a cow, an elephant, a dog, and an outcast.*
223. *When the mind is established in Unity, one conquers the problems of life and attains Brahman who is impartial and free from all coatings.*
224. *One who has realized the Brahman lives eternally in identity with Brahman and does not feel perturbed when he comes across unpleasant situations nor does he feel elated when he receives something pleasant. His intellect is firm and he is free from delusion.*
225. *As his mind is not attached to any external enjoyments he finds delight in the Self, he is able to be linked with the Supreme and derives eternal bliss.*

Now the journey really begins. Now the sense of where you are headed becomes more tangible. In your meditations, experiences are coming that strengthen this un-nameable relationship with something that has not been here before.

When all appear as equal, when one experiences the one soul in all living beings, then one has attained the state of unity with Brahman. In this state suffering ends.

The *Brahman* in Sanskrit is the truth, or the one soul from which all souls come. The soul is our individual expression of the Brahman. Becoming aware of the soul is becoming aware of yourself as the Brahman. They are the same thing.

When you break out of the box, you first notice an awareness of this inexplicable thing that is occurring in you. You may call it by different names, but it is your own experience. At this stage the tendency of your consciousness is to move into relationship with something vaster than what is in yourself. It is a spontaneous prayerful relationship. You begin to connect to that in you that is the Brahman; it automatically turns you to the universal expression of that which is manifesting in you individually. It is a concurrent action. So as you feel connected to the soul, to the silence and stillness within you, it connects you to the vast silence and stillness which is the Brahman.

Subtle universal forces take over your own individual effort. They begin to work in your system. There is an opening to something greater than yourself. There is a sense of presence, or awareness, or both, depending on whether you are more open in the heart or the mind. Every time you experience these qualities within yourself, you are actually connecting to the universal expression of those qualities. This may not yet be clear to you, but it is a beginning. You start having moments of seeing yourself in the flower, the tree, the bird, the insect. You feel yourself connecting to the presence of that which is physically in your sensory world. When that happens you are not seeing a difference between the fly on your arm, the tree, the butterfly, the bird, or the dog. They all take on a quality of expressing in their own unique way, the same quality that you are now in connection with.

"*When the mind is established in Unity*" refers to that state of awareness. The focus in the Bhagavad Gita up through Chapter 8 is on the development of that awareness. But what is going on concurrently is your ability to connect to this quality of oneness. Merging with awareness and merging with oneness go on at the same time, although you will at different times focus more on the awareness or on the experience of this connection. It is the same process. When you move into unity, there is a feeling of connecting to something greater than yourself. Prior to this you may have felt a greater peace and calmness within. Now there is a sense of connection to something larger than yourself.

You are moving into unity with something larger than that which has lived you as ego. Ultimately there comes a point when the Brahman becomes real—but that is later. In Verse 224 Krishna is describing a symptom of one who has realized the Brahman, one whose identity has become established in the universal expression of truth. That occurs later in Chapter 8. The more you are connected to this universal expression, and the firmer your determination, the stronger is your capacity to endure the distractions of the world and the resistances of your human nature. The more you are able to access this knowledge, the more fire there is in you. There is more willingness to take the action because you are beginning to experience something. This effortlessness, this actionlessness, starts coming to you, and you move with greater efficiency toward truth.

When this happens, relinquishing is natural. Renunciation is natural. You don't have to work at it. You are just no longer interested. It just doesn't pull at you any more. Like a child leaving a sandbox, playing with friends, riding a bicycle, going to a party—we just change domains. We step from a small arena of satisfaction into a much larger arena of fulfillment and satisfaction. So relinquishing is not a big deal, because we are turning away from the empty, hollow, plastic things of that small world to those things that are more real and fulfilling. You become curious and interested in that which is now unfolding. This is what defines the point of no return: a movement away from the sandbox toward the universe. It is an important and critical transition in the development of consciousness.

228. *One who finds happiness, light, and delight within himself is a true yogi, and being identified with Brahman he attains Brahman.*

229. *When sins are wiped out, doubts are dispelled, and the mind is firmly established in the Self, one attains Brahman. Such a seer is actively engaged in the welfare of all beings.*

230. *Being free from desire and anger and their thoughts controlled, they attain Brahma nirvana and there is eternal peace all around them.*

Breaking the Pull of Gravity

The state that is being described is actionlessness. It is where you are consciously or unconsciously an instrument for truth, love, and wisdom in the world. You begin to radiate something that is beyond the human through your personality, ego, mind, or actions. You are becoming more and more empty, less and less needing to have things go this way or that. But the pressure of life can still occasionally sweep you away. It is as if you are in the upper atmosphere and you drop to a lower orbit. But you are more easily pulled back into a higher orbit. You are not yet in the gravitational pull of the sun, but you are no longer bound by the gravity of the earth. There is a coming in and out of being bound, but it is of a completely different order from what you experienced before. The link has been broken; the gravity of the inclinations of human nature no longer bind you. You've moved into another paradigm of being. Yet you may not even know it consciously.

We read writings from people who have stepped out of this box, made this transition. They are expanded in their awareness yet not fully integrated. It is still coming. They may be spiritual teachers or writers. Or if you are more inclined to feeling, then it is your experience and there is no pull to write; you are only pulled to your experience of connecting to a vastness greater than yourself. You only know that you love this feeling that is occurring, this thing that is rising up in your body. It grows more and more. You don't always hear about those people because they have no need to share it, to intellectualize, to articulate, to define; but they are in the same state of consciousness. And when you are around those people you feel lifted, freer, calmer, and are drawn to them without knowing why. There is something simple, attractive, and innocent in them.

232. *The sage who has brought his senses, mind, and intellect under control, from whom desire, fear, and anger have vanished, is liberated while living.*

233. *Knowing Me in reality as the goal of all sacrifices and austerities, the Lord of all the worlds and the Friend of all beings; one attains supreme peace.*

These last verses lead us into Chapter 6. You turn your consciousness away from the world toward that which you are now experiencing. You move away from the distractions of the outer world and focus attention on the inner connection. That is what we will be addressing in the next chapter, The Yoga of Meditation.

The Yoga of Meditation

Yoga is that state when the mind becomes silent
and still and the self is satisfied by seeing the Self
and derives delight from the Self.
∽ VERSE 253

In the sixth chapter we are now moving into a direct relationship with the soul. We are exploring the state of consciousness and the means of reaching the state of consciousness called meditation. Meditation is the indicator and also the technique of moving into oneness with the soul, of moving into relationship with the essential quality that lives us. Meditation is basically contemplation of that which contemplates, when our conscious attention starts turning from an outwardly to an inwardly oriented focus. This inward orientation isn't just on mind, thoughts, memories, moods, and feelings. It is on something more essential. It starts turning its attention to that which is the source of attention. This chapter gives techniques for finding the consciousness that lives us.

The Movement of Consciousness

Due to the nature of consciousness, we are all born with a tendency to look outward. It is the inclination of consciousness to turn outward. We put our attention on the internal thoughts associated with outward relationships and the feelings associated with those thoughts. We tend to become preoccupied with our thoughts and moods associated with suffering. So there has to be something other than suffering in us that awakens. Without a connection to an inner quality of being, we wouldn't have any inclination toward meditation. In order to meditate we must already be in a relatively mature state of consciousness.

The Hindus have two terms for the movement of consciousness. *Pravritti* is the tendency of consciousness to grow and evolve outwardly, the inclination that takes one toward objects of pleasure. And *nivritti* is the tendency of consciousness to turn inwardly, the inclination that takes one away from objects of pleasure. Nivritti is consciousness returning to its origin.

For consciousness to turn inward there has to be a motive, something inside that becomes aware of itself. As we have seen, that process is one of dejection, discrimination, action, knowledge, and renunciation. This is a movement from fascination with the world of mind, senses, moods, reactions, and feelings to that which is the source of those things. It doesn't happen naturally. If it hadn't been for the process discussed in the previous five chapters, the consciousness would not easily turn inward to the Self. It is not a natural movement. Natural movements are like the rest of nature—outwardly oriented absorption with the objects of pleasure, the senses, the body and material life.

The first technique the Gita gives us is sense control. If you don't make an effort to control the senses, consciousness will jump to whatever objects the senses focus on. Without sense control, meditation is not possible. Unless we restrain the inclination of the senses to jump outward to seek fulfillment, we cannot do this journey. The outward orientation of consciousness is very unstable, it jumps from one thing to another. Meditation is about becoming stable, to stop jumping, to become still. When we develop enough sense control, then what happens naturally is that the mind, the instrument of the five senses, automatically grows quiet and still. That is the beginning of the preparation for yoga.

When the mind starts quieting, the vital, the emotions, and the action drives also start quieting. In the Gita the path of quieting the mind is taking action without attachment to an outcome, without an investment with the results or the process of obtaining that result. Training yourself to act without attachment to the outcome purifies and quiets the vital. When the vital begins to quiet, then what happens naturally is that the consciousness turns to the truth of the Self, one's inner being. This is the process that we call the Yoga of Knowledge. This knowledge gives us a sense of the quality of being that is more present and able to turn inward. When this happens, the inclination to go outward starts quieting. Through meditation, consciousness is ready to collaborate with this inward orientation.

Meditation is a movement into relationship with that which is the soul, the truth of the Self, the essence of the Self. Consciousness turns inward on itself. For some people, it comes naturally. They sit and automatically become quiet and contemplative. They turn inward and the world falls away. Often people who can meditate already have a capacity to be single-focused, a capacity to have a purpose and to organize life around that. But for most, these qualities need to be developed.

DIFFERENT TYPES OF MEDITATION

There are basically three types of meditation, just as there are three gunas. Tamasic meditation is sleep and stupor, zoned out, not paying attention, only partially present. Rajasic meditation is simply being miserable, sitting with restlessness, with endlessly changing thoughts, and desiring to be doing anything but meditating. Sattwic meditation is the only natural meditation. When someone is sufficiently sattwic, then it comes naturally. This capacity to meditate may be in the mental, or in the vital (in the drives and feelings), or in the body. It could be in all three, or any two, or any one.

The ability to be contemplative, in relationship with the present moment, exists within all living creatures. It is only human beings that isolate themselves from that natural repose, or presence with what is arising. Animals and plants are in constant relationship with what they are and the world about them, although they don't know it. Unlike the rest of nature, human beings can separate themselves from what they are and become miserable as a consequence, thinking they are a "who," not a "what," making stories, striving and being dissatisfied.

Here in the West there are many different choices of meditation: Vipassana, Buddhist, or Christian; focusing meditations or imagination-based meditations. But if your system is not prepared, you won't be able to meditate for very long. Maybe you will have five minutes, ten minutes, or fifteen minutes max. Only when you have been organizing your life in order to move into relationship with the soul can meditation become a natural part of your daily experience.

In this chapter Krishna is revealing to Arjuna something of the nature of meditation and also meditation as a technique for moving toward the truth of the soul, hinting at its relationship with Samadhi and equanimity, and other attributes described in earlier chapters. Meditation is the maturation, the settling down of the otherwise restless consciousness, becoming silent and still.

Let's begin with Chapter 6, The Yoga of Meditation (Dhyana Yoga).

The Blessed Lord said:

234. *One who performs his ordained duties without expecting the fruits of action is a true sannyasi and a yogi, but not the one who has given up the rituals or outer activities.*
235. *Arjuna, what is called sannyasa is also known as yoga because no one can ever become a yogi without renouncing desire.*

Two basic principles of the Bhagavad Gita are reviewed here. When applied, they allow us to rest. The first is detachment from the outcome of our actions. When you let go of needing the meditation to produce a certain kind of outcome, or let go of whatever else you could be doing besides meditating, you become poised in relationship with the present moment. The second is renouncing desire: sannyasa, letting go of having things different than they are, letting go of endless striving. The human ego is endlessly restless, desiring certain outcomes or desiring things to be different than they are. So when we have consciously quieted these things, then meditation comes more naturally.

The self and the Self

238. *The Self is said to be the friend and also the enemy of the self. Therefore, one should liberate the self by the help of the Self and not bind it by the self.*

Here the Gita speaks of the relationship of two selves. The capital "S" Self is our authentic Self. It is that quality of our identity, aligned with the spiritual path, which has an inherent intelligence and will without human conditioning and attachment. This verse is referring to letting go of the human ego, the small "s" self, and moving into relationship with our inner being as a collaborator rather than as an enemy. Our human nature moves into alignment with our spiritual nature. We come out of our identification with the ego and move into relationship with that central quality of being which is the essence of what we are. This is the eternal Self.

This Self is the organizing principle of all human beings that gives us self-awareness. Inherent in it is intelligence, curiosity, and a capacity for action. And it has an ability to choose. This is the "what" behind the "who" that is doing the yoga. This Self comes forward the more we do yoga. The part of the human ego that is not aligned with it falls away as our human nature becomes more aligned with this central Self and starts becoming more and more like it. This eternal unchanging awareness that does not change but is embodied is called the *jivatman.* It is the portion of the Self that has taken on the identity of an individual in a body.

This sense of identity that is organizing around the personal self is a reflection of the principle of "I am." This "I am-ness" is a characteristic of the big Self. It is what asks questions that take actions. It is that organizing principle around which our ego, the little self, has shaped itself. The central Self is silent and still; it rests in the background, giving or withdrawing its consent to get involved or not, to act or not. When there is a spiritual experience, insight, inspiration, or aspiration, we connect to this big Self. It enlivens and enriches the little self, the ego. But then it recedes. Why? Because the little self is not yet the friend of the big Self, is not organized to hold this experience.

THE SELF: FRIEND OR FOE OF THE EGO?

239. *One who has conquered the self by the Self, for him the self is a friend, but one who is unable to do this, for him the self is like an enemy.*

The ego is made up of multiple selves. It is just a structure of repetitive habits—of thinking and feeling associated with the body—held together by a shallow sense of self. Ego says, "This is me. This is my thought. This is my feeling." Each becomes a differing point of view that shapes how the world shows up for us. Imagine a cluster of multiple selves in which there is a central seat. Whoever is in the central seat runs the show. If you are in a bad mood, then other parts of this self align with the bad mood. If the good mood comes forward, then all the other parts align with that. You, the ego, the personality, don't notice the difference. You don't question this; it is just accepted as the way it is. Who is in the driver's seat? We think that whoever is running the show is us. We think that all the parts aligned with whoever is in the driver's seat is us. This is ego, the error of the separate little self.

When in a good mood, all these parts of our identity are in a good mood and we feel good. And when in a bad mood, it's all crap. There is not a center; there is no ground of being. Until the Self starts coming forward—giving the little self the ability to apply effort and discipline, to set a goal or create a purpose—the human ego, the little self, will be in chaos. You have to have the boss come forward and take a stand and say, "Hey you guys, get your act together. We are up to something. We aren't just going this way and that way." The boss starts kicking ass and telling the different parts of yourself to get their act together. The boss applies intelligence to reach its purpose. The true Self is the boss. By the sixth chapter the boss has come forward.

240. *One who has conquered his self attains peace and calmness,*
   remains unperturbed by heat or cold, pain or pleasure,
   praise or censure.

When the boss comes forward, it is not fooled by all the multiple little selves, scrabbling and irritated, or maybe happy and liking the control, depending on their mood. It doesn't lose itself in each of its points of view. It is the director of the play. The old self may say, "We were running this kingdom just fine before you showed up. Why don't you just go away?" Or, "We like what you are saying. We'll go along with it." It depends on which of our multiple selves are in alignment. The positive part of the self tends to be more aligned with the Self. The self is the friend of the Self. The negative self tends to resist and oppose, to be more aligned in its unhappy smallness, dissatisfaction, complaint, and negativity. The self here is the enemy of the Self. There is a battle going on until enough parts align with the prompting of the true Self.

So the Self can be the friend and also the enemy. If the little self doesn't want to cooperate, watch out. Like a recalcitrant child resisting change to its habits, it can be stubborn and rebellious. But the boss will kick ass. Eventually the boss will win. Why? Because it is closer to truth. It is only the authentic Self, the boss, that can do this yoga. If you let the little self have its way you will be diminished, you will lose your authority and power to let go, to choose, to create. When the boss comes forward, the discordant parts of yourself begin to quiet and become obedient. When that happens, all parts of the self start quieting. The stubborn parts let go. And you find yourself in the state of meditation.

241. *A yogi who has conquered his self is ever satisfied with knowledge and wisdom and is free from aversion; for him a stone, gold, and a lump of earth are of equal importance.*

When the Self comes forward, it brings with it an authority, an organizing principle. When the best parts of your ego align with the Self, then peace and calmness come. We find our center; we ground into our being. We find that it is this central Self that has been doing our yoga all along; it is what motivated us to apply effort, to change and discover this quality of being. It is what has been living us all along. You are at the threshold of realizing this. At this point you may have been doing yoga for years. You are able to let go of your attachment to outcomes, to relinquish your position, to not go into a negative story or point of view. Your little self is merging with the eternal Self. It has gained some authority over your little self. I call this our authentic Self.

242. *A yogi who has reached a higher state accepts all equally, whether they are well-wishers, friends, enemies, persons of indifference, mediators, relatives, saints, or even sinners.*

This is the state of equality where the consciousness is fulfilled being with itself. The tendency to assign value or importance to things lessens. The nature of ego is that it makes things important or unimportant to itself. But to the authentic Self they are all interesting, they are all equal in importance. There is an ability to accept whatever is arising—whether difficult, confusing, and uncomfortable, or easy, illuminating, and satisfying. They are all seen as equal expressions of the same thing. When one reaches this state, value is not assigned to anything outside. Because you are beginning to draw nurturance and fulfillment from within, the need for fulfillment from outside lessens automatically.

You don't need to have anything in order to be fulfilled. You don't need to avoid anything in order to feel peace and calmness. This is the quality of one who has come to the state of the stitha prajna, the state of equanimity. It is the state of equality. Desire has quieted, the pull to the world of senses, the mind has become quiet and still. All is now equal. These qualities are reflective of one who has reached one's own orbit, one who has come to the point of no return. The old ways can still come forward, but you are no longer overtaken. This capacity to see your beliefs and positions about yourself and outward things allows them to fade in their ability to rule you. You become more filled just being and not needing to have an opinion or a judgment, not needing to know or strive or resist.

TECHNIQUES OF MEDITATION

In this chapter Krishna is giving a set of specific instructions in Verses 243 through 246. There are only about three or four places that have specific instructions but nothing as specific about the technology of meditation as in this chapter. Elsewhere there are only hints. And these instructions are given just as Arjuna is about to participate in killing 16 million people. So what is this role of meditation relative to where we are headed? You will notice that someone like Arjuna, who is rajasic and inclined to fight, does not find meditation natural. It was clear that Arjuna needed some specific help, because he wasn't going to get there based on his warrior nature. He needed specific information about how to redesign his relationship with his true nature.

243. *While practicing the yoga of ceaseless union with the Self, one should avoid crowded places and try to live within, banishing all ideas of material possession. One should also remain free from desire and control the senses.*

This verse begins with basic instructions. *"Avoid crowded places."* The environment influences your consciousness. The habit of the consciousness is to get distracted by a disruptive environment. *"Try to live within."* You need a relatively quiet place to become aware of your body, of you in your body, and of you breathing in your body. You are moving inward. *"Banish all ideas of material possession."* Remove distractions of the things that you have to do, the things you are attached to, the things you worry about, the things you have planned for. Consciously let go of those things in this period of meditation. *"Remain free from desire and control the senses."* The mind, which is the organizing principle of the senses, tends to be constantly activated. You withdraw all thoughts from anything that would have you be other than where you are right now. You let go of the desire to be someone else. You let go of the desire of all the things you had to do before or after meditation. You don't let yourself get hooked into the impact of a thought that arises. You are learning to bring the boss forward, the true Self forward in the moment of meditation.

244. *For practicing the yoga of meditation one should select a serene place and prepare a comfortable and stable seat.*

This verse offers more specifics. Find a designated place in your house, or if in a spiritual community, then in the meditation hall, where you meditate. When you first begin to meditate it is very difficult. But when you meditate in the same place on a regular basis, something of that orientation becomes more readily available to you. Sit in a comfortable and relaxed position. It is not necessary to be upright, rigid, and uncomfortable. Many techniques of meditation are organized to keep you alert so you don't fall asleep. But the Gita says what is needed is just a comfortable and stable seat so you can feel held in your position and not worry about falling over or collapsing. I recommend that people sit up 45 degrees or more, so you can be reclined. Beyond that point people tend to go into a stupor.

245. *Sitting on such a seat, one should try to concentrate on the Self by controlling the mind and the senses.*

Turning your attention from outward things, pulling your attention away from your thoughts and the things that are going on, try to find that connection with the soul that has been your guidepost along these previous five chapters. As you move into that quietude or connection, you may experience this in the body, or in the vital, or in the awareness. You may feel your body growing quiet as you begin to pay attention to what is going on with you inwardly. Or you may feel the restlessness in your vital growing quiet or feel something happening in your heart.

For most people, it is experienced in their awareness. There is a progressive quieting of the distractibility of the consciousness that goes into mind and thinking. You are becoming aware that thoughts are going on where before you were your thoughts. I call it a silence and stillness practice. You are looking to find that in you which is silent and still. What you are connecting with is stability, not instability. You are looking to connect with that stability which is still and silent. This is the thread that allows meditation to become a meaningful practice in your life.

246. *While meditating, one should ensure that the neck, body and spine are erect and motionless, the consciousness is fixed inward on the Self and the thoughts are not desultory.*

The neck, body, and spine should be erect and not crouched over or bent to the side. But if you are meditating on your own, it is useful to make sure that whatever position you are in, the head, neck, and body are aligned if you are reclining. Inevitably if you go into a deep meditation the body will move. Your head may fall forward, but then you are in deep meditation, so you don't need to worry about this.

The Samadhi State

247. *In order to attain the samadhi state through meditation one should have inner calmness, be free from fear and firmly follow the vow of celibacy; by controlling the mind the seeker should concentrate on Me only and accept Me as his supreme goal.*

In this verse samadhi is mentioned for the first time since the second chapter. Krishna says that if you want to attain samadhi, then this is what you do. Not everyone wants to attain samadhi. Some people meditate just to feel good and have more peace and happiness. But some people feel the pull to a more profound relationship with their soul, their essential Self. Samadhi is not possible unless there is a significant degree of inner calmness. The vow of celibacy is very important, because the inclination of the body to get caught up in male or female sexual energy is very distracting and gripping. Samadhi cannot take root when the sexual nature is still active.

"Controlling the mind the seeker should concentrate on Me only and accept Me as his supreme goal." Where did this "Me" come in? Weren't we trying to find the soul? Who is this Me? Sounds like Krishna. This is where we begin to understand the relationship between Krishna and Arjuna. Who is Krishna for Arjuna? What is Krishna? Is there such a thing as a Krishna within? We begin to step out of this conversation of impersonality and move into relationship to something that is within us that is greater than what we can know as ourselves.

In the West this merger with the Self is the most commonly recognized state of realization. It is a movement from identification with moods and whims and stories to that which is the essence of your existence. You live in the now. You are in presence. What you are is that which is presence. It is the ability to realize the Self within. It may get veiled or clouded, but it has become a permanent part of everyday life, something that is there multiple times in the day. It is a constant organizing presence for you. This Self-realization is the first attainment.

250. *Yoga removes all sorrow from one who is temperate in food and recreation, is self-controlled, detached from the fruits of work, and who has regulated his sleep and waking state.*

The asceticism that was required in Chapters 4 and 5 is no longer needed. Yoga becomes more relaxed, although you still avoid activities that obscure consciousness. You enjoy activities that enhance consciousness, and you therefore naturally move into harmony with life and existence. Things are more effortless. It is less of you that is applying effort. These are all symptomatic of one who has come to a stable relationship with the Self, the Krishna within.

In this state a quality of balance and peacefulness comes. There is not as much struggle, not as much fighting against your willfulness, desires, habits, or inclinations. You are moving to a place where you can be more relaxed, more joyful, more curious. It is a state of being where you are not perturbed. In the gunas this would be the sattwa state of consciousness that is attached to happiness and knowledge, the enjoyment of existence.

251. *When the seeker, through controlled mind, develops a natural dispassion for objects of pleasure and his consciousness rests only on the Self, he attains the yoga siddhi state.*

The *yoga siddhi* state means the yoga has come to its first completion. The separate consciousness has moved into relationship with that which is the source of it, the Self. The ego has merged into this condition of being. This is the attainment. That is what siddhi means. When this is there naturally, then you are a master of meditation and yoga. It is the first true proof, the first true shift.

This happens spontaneously for some people. They step out of their identification with ego and become that which has an ego. They step out of their identification with their moods or thoughts and become that which has a mood or thoughts. For most people it is a gradual process. The being comes forward, and it comes more and more forward until it is taken for granted. It is your everyday normal existence. This is the yoga siddhi that this chapter is pointing to.

252. *Like the flame of the lamp that does not flicker when pro-*
tected from the wind, the mind of a yogi at this stage is not
perturbed since it is united with the Self.

Quiet, at peace, calm, fulfilled within itself, nothing missing, nothing needed. But this realization is still in the mental plane, in the awareness. It is not fully established in the rest of the system. It is an awareness that you are that which is the source of awareness. It is not necessarily that there are not moods or bad days or desires, but you become relaxed and okay with yourself and life. Why? Because without thinking you know how to respond to the situations that arise. You know when to apply effort and when not to apply effort. You become more happy and successful.

You may not even know you have come to this state. Meditation comes naturally, and there is a love of spiritual things. Here in the West there are quite a few who come to the state of the Self and don't even know it or else take it for granted. It may not be a big deal for one who has already attained this state. That is why these first six chapters are preparatory, taking one out of identification with human consciousness into becoming identified with consciousness itself. Many on the path are in various stages in this journey. But it is still not integral. It still hasn't come into its full power and significance.

The Bliss of Meditation

254. *Yoga is that state when the yogi experiences endless bliss*
that results from a purified intellect but not from sense
contact; once established in this state, the yogi is not likely
to fall from the truth of the Self.

This state of endless bliss is the result of lots of meditation. Endless bliss occurs when the outer self begins to move into relationship with the inner self. This is why meditation is so enchanting when the consciousness gets to a certain point. With sufficient self-discipline the consciousness starts quieting and becomes receptive and begins to experience its own nature. That experience of its own nature is bliss. Meditation is the means of becoming more established in the state of the point of no return. The point of no return was described in Chapter 5 as where the consciousness overcomes the pull of the outer inclinations and reaches its own orbit. It was wavering in a lower orbit but has reached a point where it does not drop to earth as readily. It has achieved a state of detachment and witnessing.

Meditation is a powerful tool for stabilizing the consciousness in its own orbit. One is not likely to fall from the truth of the Self once established in the state of meditation. The bliss that comes in meditation is more fulfilling than an outer bliss, which is temporary and inevitably creates suffering. The Gita says, *"No other gain is considered greater and one is not shaken even by profoundest sorrow."* In yoga, moving into relationship with that quality of being that we are in truth is the purpose and the fulfillment of this yoga. This chapter is pointing to the individual state of the Self, the individual realization of being.

Our individual being is part, or one aspect, of a vast beingness. We are all individual expressions of one beingness, and we each move in connection with our own beingness. We then begin to move into relationship with beingness everywhere and in all things. This brings peace and bliss. It is also the beginning of the end of fear, desire, and anger. Instead of being in reactivity, fear, and defensiveness with others, we begin to move into empathy and connection with the being in others. We are not caught in that endless cycle of ego protecting itself or enhancing itself, because we have found another Self to rest within.

Meditation—A Means to the Self

256. *This state of sorrowless union is called yoga and one should practice this tirelessly with strong determination.*

Persistent effort is the key to becoming established in the state of merger with the Self. This is the purpose of this stage of the journey, the yoga of meditation. The goal is to become one with the Self. Meditation is the means to have this happen. The closer one comes to the Self, the more increasingly effective is the meditation. This is the evidence that one's consciousness has matured. Meditation becomes natural. It is all you want to do. To sit may still take effort initially, but in time it becomes easier and easier. This process simultaneously strengthens your ability to detach from the outward world, your emotions, and inner thoughts. It brings you into a state of greater quiet, peace, and bliss.

257. *How to practice yoga? First, abandon all desire-prompted thoughts and control the senses by the mind.*

In meditation there is a series of stages. At first your thoughts will become apparent to you, where before you were your thoughts. When you become aware of your thoughts, you become aware of the misery of being stuck in your thoughts, where before you didn't notice. The inclination of thoughts is to drive you to action, so you are not aware of being caught up in your thoughts. That is why self-control is so necessary at this stage. It allows you to just sit with the thoughts and not act on them. You learn not to lose yourself in thoughts of the past or projections into the future. You learn how to bring yourself to the present. Without this effort you will be caught up in your thoughts every time you meditate, and you will either become so restless that you can't meditate, or you will just lose consciousness and fall asleep.

The ability to break free from the pull of your thoughts and not go where they lead brings forward a new kind of authority, a quality of being that comes from the soul itself. This authority enhances your ability to go beyond the inclinations of the ego. The more you apply this authority, the more ability you have to witness and be present with the thoughts without being overtaken by them. You begin to experience the state of thoughtlessness—being without thinking. You discover a state that is both silent and still. The uncomfortable quality that thoughts bring begins to quiet. You can start seeing thoughts passing through your field of consciousness with more detachment. You move into a place where you can witness thinking going on. You discover that you have some power over those thoughts; whereas when they are closer to you, you don't have much say and have to endure them calmly.

258. *Slowly dive deep into the state of tranquility by holding the mind under firm intellect. Immerse in the Self and remain there for as long as possible without inviting any thought.*

The first stage of meditation is this awareness of thoughts. The ability to tolerate being with thoughts and not being overtaken by them leads to a state of calmness. The next stage is silence, which deepens into stillness. Silence and stillness take us to a state of peace. Peace deepens and brings us to bliss. This is a process. It takes a consecrated effort, every day over time, often for years.

The first stage of meeting the automatic thinking mechanism can be discouraging. Yet only by learning to sit in meditation can you get the ability to break the habit of identifying with your thoughts. But in time you do gain increasing authority over them. They no longer take you down the rabbit hole of your stories and habitual patterns of thinking. The more you sit, the more capacity you have to witness and to dismiss thoughts;

to not go where they are trying to take you. Those who sit for an hour or so regularly usually can come to the state of calmness at some point. The very act of applying effort to sit still strengthens the capacity to move into this state of meditation.

As this state of meditation strengthens, you move into a state of silence. You will notice either there are no thoughts, or if there are thoughts, you are not noticing them. There is an overall sense of silence, and it is easier to sit still for long periods of time. The body is less restless; you become more comfortable. You are not as sensitive to external noises as you were. As silence and stillness deepens, then there is a sense of peace, as if the quietude of your mind is sinking into your whole body. By the time peacefulness occurs, the consciousness is beginning to be rhythmic rather than restless. Silence and peace are maybe indistinguishable, but peace is more in the body. Silence is more in the mind.

"Immerse in the Self and remain there for as long as possible." When you reach a state of calmness, the best way to strengthen your ability to attain those states as part of your outward life is to stay in those states as long as possible. That is how you train the habit of your restless consciousness to be more calm and tranquil. If you come out of meditation in calmness, you won't immediately go back into your thoughts. If you get into silence, there will be an inclination to remain silent, and you will be calmer in your outer life. If you get into the state of peace without any effort on your part, there is an inward silence, no matter what outward activity you are doing. And if you reach the state of bliss, you will stay in peace, even when you engage in outer action.

As peace deepens, there comes an experience of bliss. When bliss comes, you are actually experiencing the state of the Self. That is the goal of this chapter: to reach this state of merger with the Self. It becomes easy and natural to stay in it as long as possible. This tends to quiet the perturbations of your spiritual struggle and make meditation effortless. The Gita says to *"dive deep into the state of tranquility"*; so let yourself dive deep past the restless thoughts and into the deeper states of silence, stillness, peace, and bliss. This is the state of tranquility.

259. *Mind is by nature fickle, it wanders away and wavers; therefore, one should always bring the mind to the Self alone.*

Meditation is a means of connecting to the Self. In time, it will bring an inner silence, stillness and peace into your daily life. This brings one to the state of stitha prajna. This occurs when one is merged with the Self. The consciousness has become stable, even when engaged in action. One is now able to bring the state of meditation into one's life. The individual consciousness is merged with the Self. One is now capable of being fully present with what is arising. Your attachment for action quiets as a consequence of your ability to keep that connection with the Self. The mind is the obstacle of meditation because it serves the ego, the separate self. But once one's identity moves from the self to the Self, the mind loses its power. The consciousness has reached maturity. Meditation is now natural and spontaneous.

260. *The yogi who is tranquil in mind and free from the perturbation of rajas and the impurity of tamas, dwells in supreme bliss and enjoys the delight of the Brahman.*

When we merge with this higher Self within ourselves, we are also meeting the universal being, the Brahman. Your individual quality of being connects you to the universal quality of being. At this stage this is primarily occurring in our upper chakras, the part of the awareness associated with the upper body. It is not yet integrated throughout the emotions and the body. But it is with this attainment that we can establish a foundation upon which we can move into a deeper relationship with this Self, the essence of ourselves.

261. *Thus freed from the stains of passion and remaining con-*
stantly in yoga, the yogi easily attains the delight of the
infinite bliss of the Brahman.

The efforts that have been made before—through discrimination, action, knowledge, and renunciation—take you
away from the inclination of reactivity and addiction and
strengthen your ability to relinquish those things in your life
that are not true. Each helps the other. Now at this point the
yoga of meditation is one of the most powerful and effective
means that have been described up until now in the Gita. But
it takes time. You have to establish yourself in this state. You
have to consciously strive to remain in this state, to bring
it forward in your own day-to-day experience, so that it is a
tangible reality for you.

In order to become established in this state, it is important
to be in or create the right environment for yourself. It is important initially to avoid undue distractions from your outer life by
removing yourself from unnecessary obligations and responsibilities, distractions from the past due to family, relationships,
and friends, and letting go of any remaining attachments. All
the previous chapters are the foundation for allowing this state
to establish itself. It is critical to stay focused. Yet some actions
in the world are needed to help test, integrate, and strengthen
this state in oneself. The more you become established in the
Self, the less likely you will be overtaken when you do step out
of your protected environment. Ultimately you will need to step
out. Arjuna is going to fight a battle filled with all its horrific
activity. For him to stay detached from the outcome, he will
need to be firmly established in this state of yoga.

262. *Such a yogi sees all in the Self and the Self in all.*
263. *One who sees Me in all and all beings in Me, to him I am*
always visible and to Me he is also always visible.

This practice of meditation is an action, an effort to restrain the inclination to do other things. Yoga is action that takes you to the goal of yoga. By disciplining yourself in order to meditate, you have reached a state of very effective action. This ability to move into relationship with the inner being through meditation and to come to that dynamic inner relationship with the Self, no matter what is going on outwardly, is the highest state of attainment in the Gita up to now. When we move into relationship with the Self, the source of our beingness and existence, we automatically begin to move into relationship with the one universal being of which we are all individual expressions.

Moving Into the Universal

264. *The yogi who worships Me and loves Me as one in every being, without discrimination, is always present in Me, whatever may be his mode of life.*
265. *Arjuna, a supreme yogi views the pain and pleasure of others with empathy while seeing the same Self everywhere.*

In this chapter the being within is beginning to move into relationship with the being without. It is the beginning of this recognition of the universal by the individual. The individual is moving in relationship with the universal. *"One who sees Me in all and all beings in Me"*—the Me in this case is the universal aspect that Krishna represents. When you move into that in yourself, you automatically move into relationship with the Krishna principle, or the divine principle, or Brahman. When you find it within yourself, you automatically start seeing it elsewhere.

This moving into relationship with the being both inside yourself and outside yourself will be the movement that takes the realization from the individual self to God. The spiritual journey has stages: From ego to Self, from Self to God, and from God to Truth. In these chapters we are talking about the journey from ego to Self. At the end of this chapter we are beginning the journey from Self to God.

When one comes to relationship with the Self, what happens is very magical: You change your paradigm. Your ability to experience the subtle vibrations of existence gets enhanced. Things like mantra, music, chants, or the ability to feel spiritual energy from others becomes available to you.

You begin to experience Existence, not just through the five senses, but through a huge array of possible sources of experiencing the subtle worlds. It is the indication that one has come to the Self when one starts to feel these subtle energies. Through mantra and chanting there can be a sensation of energy felt in your heart, in your awareness, or in your body. If this has happened, then you can know that the Self is awakened in you. You are beginning to experience the universe in its true quality, free of the limitation of the mind and five senses. You are experiencing energy. This feeling quality of energy and this awareness quality of energy is the domain that you are now entering into at this stage of the Gita.

QUIETING THE FICKLE MIND

Arjuna said:

266. *Krishna, this yoga, which presupposes even-mindedness, appears to be an impossible proposition to me because my mind is so fickle.*
267. *My mind is so restless, turbulent, stormy, and obstinate. It seems to me as difficult to control it as the wind.*

At this point of the Gita Arjuna has enough self-awareness to know his mind runs him. I meet so many people who say they cannot meditate, or even sit still for ten minutes without getting restless. And even when they do try to meditate, their mind is unruly and uncontrollable. Sometimes it is easy and natural to meditate, but usually effort is required, especially at first.

These verses point out the necessity of effort. Whatever has come to Arjuna is not yet stable enough in his body. Meditation is the technique to embed it more deeply in him. This discipline of sitting still and becoming aware of oneself as a field of consciousness is a way to accelerate the quieting of the mind and system, but it takes persistence and detachment from the outcome. Otherwise you are likely to become discouraged and give up. But you need to resist this impulse. This is especially hard if you are in rajas. Rajas makes you feel so restless that sitting quiet and still seems impossible. Yet that is when you have to apply discipline to keep sitting.

The Blessed Lord said:

268. *This yoga, Arjuna, may be difficult at the beginning, but through constant practice and dispassion one can be successful in it.*
269. *Yes, I agree, this yoga is difficult for him whose mind is not controlled, but if one strives hard with perseverance it is attainable.*

So Krishna is reassuring Arjuna that through persistence and effort he will be able to conquer this inclination of his mind. At times meditation will be easier, at times it will be harder. When it is harder you have to reject your mind's story that it is not working. Of course, at times you will just go unconscious and become obscured. This is due to the waves of sattwa, rajas, and tamas that we cycle through every day. When you are in sattwa, meditation is more natural. When you are in rajas, you can meditate but it is a lot of work. In tamas you feel completely obscured—there is no connection, there is nothing happening or you go unconscious. However, often going unconscious due to a tamas cycle is not the same as one who is receiving so much force that they lose outer consciousness. They are in fact in a deep state of merger in which their body seems to be asleep.

Meditation comes more naturally in sattwa. But by controlling the senses, there will be less domination by rajas. By restraining the impulse for action you will be converting the rajas into sattwa. By strengthening the sattwa and restraining the rajas you will reduce the tamas automatically. Whenever you take action aligned with sattwa, the rajas and tamas automatically reduce. This is what Krishna means when he says, *"But if one strives hard with perseverance it is attainable."*

THE NECESSITY OF FAITH

Arjuna said:

270. *Krishna, what happens to a yogi who is not able to reach the goal due to his wavering mind, even though he has faith and interest in sadhana?*
271. *Is he likely to lose both worlds and, like a detached cloud, be blown over from the path of Brahman?*

Arjuna is speaking from his mental consciousness. His intelligence is aware of what Krishna described to him but it hasn't become part of his experience. He is saying, "Will this really work? What if it doesn't work and I lose the world I have plus any other world that is possible?" This is the cost-benefit calculation of every ego. Is it worth the effort? This is attachment to outcome. All doubt arises from ego's calculations, thinking it is not worth the effort.

272. *My doubt about this can be removed only by You; please guide me correctly on this point.*

But Arjuna does have faith in Krishna. He is saying, *"My doubt about this can only be removed by You."* What removes doubt? Faith. Faith is the ability to be connected to that which you are seeking even when there is no evidence. With faith comes trust and belief, but faith is first. Without faith, this path is impossible. Faith arises from the quality of your being that in its essence knows the truth. So it is a movement from now to a future point that is known through the ability to access your being. By connecting to your being you are moving into a relationship with the goal of your yoga.

Faith is knowing that something is true. When you are in sattwa, faith is strong. In rajas it is distracted. In tamas it has failed. Having access to your faith, in this case by having a Krishna, allows Arjuna to move outside of those veils and be reminded of what he really is. This quality of faith comes naturally more and more as we move into relationship with the Self. Fewer assurances are needed; there is a greater recognition of the truth that is being revealed.

FALLEN YOGIS

The Blessed Lord said:

273. *One who falls from the path of this yoga shall not be destroyed either in this life or hereafter because one who pursues the path of yoga never comes to grief.*

Here Krishna is indulging Arjuna. He is responding to his ego, reassuring him that he will not be lost. Any action done sincerely in this yoga will not be lost. This is a restatement of the wisdom he gave in Chapter 2. *"In this approach there is no loss, nor fear of contrary result, nor is there any apprehension of incurring sin. Even a little progress saves one from great fear."* Why is that? Because in this teaching there is an intellectual clarity about the goal, where with other paths this is often not the case. You may be doing techniques, performing ceremonies, performing acts of devotion, or having spiritual experiences with no sense of a goal. You are likely to be going this way and that, losing your momentum in the endless distractions of the spiritual path. If the only purpose of a tradition is to keep you in the tradition, you will just be stuck in a cyclic pattern moving from high to low and back again. You will be stuck, not knowing what to do next. But those traditions that have intellectual clarity can take you to the goal, and this focus allows you to go beyond the inevitable distractions that can occur on the spiritual path.

274. *A fallen yogi goes to the world of the righteous and dwelling there for long years he again takes birth in the family of the pure and prosperous.*
275. *Or he may be born again in the family of seers, full of wisdom and spirituality. Such a rebirth is rare in this world.*
276. *There he gets back the spiritual attainment of the previous birth and strives more intensely for perfection.*

The teachings of the Gita tell us that when you do this yoga sincerely, you are not likely to fall. Even if you don't complete the goal in a lifetime, the Gita says in the second chapter, the soul is reborn again and again. The very essence of our being, our central Self, evolves as it goes from one life to another. Even if you fall in this lifetime, you will recover what you have attained. It will come to you naturally. You will be born into a favorable circumstance for your consciousness to rise to a higher state of receptivity and recover itself. In astrology this is reflected in the Saturn return. The planet Saturn takes approximately 24 to 30 years to return to its original position. Astrologers say that until a person has had their first Saturn return, they have not yet recovered all the qualities that they developed in previous lives. All those qualities have to come to fruition before you can go beyond what you have attained in your previous life.

This is the same principle here. Anything in truth found is not lost. When you make an effort to connect to your inner being, you will be able to recover it more quickly. When you recover it there will be a greater vigor and purposefulness to recover it completely. There will be a drive, an aspiration or longing to recover what you have known from the past life. Anytime a true seeker comes to me, I can always tell that what they have is either from this life's effort or their accomplishment from a previous life. I can see it in their aspiration. I can see it in the quickness of their ability to respond, their quickness to gather information and their effectiveness in putting it into practice.

277. *Such a fallen yogi will be driven to the path of yoga by the force of circumstances due to his previous practice and goes above the range of scriptures quickly.*

278. *That yogi pursues the path of yoga with diligence and sincerity and is purified from all karmas accumulated in the course of several births, finally culminating in the highest state of bliss.*

We can't lose these qualities because they are the essential qualities of our being, the consciousness of our Self. The inner being does not forget that. The ego is nothing but the instrument for the being to express itself in this dimension. When the ego knows the being, it doesn't forget it. It becomes more open, intelligent, receptive, and capable than an ego that never met the being. That is the assurance within these verses. You can look within yourself and if this is the case for you.

In some cases, poverty, strife, cruelty, or ignorance can make it more difficult to recover our past attainment. But even in these obscuring environments we can see a being push through. Sometimes there is one member of a family that breaks out with a startling capacity to break free of these influences and create a positive life. They usually bring with them a positive attitude, an ability to recover quickly and not be so overtaken by environmental factors. They are able to overcome adversity, difficulties, and limitations much more quickly than others in the family.

In the West, with its level of prosperity, security, and comfort unheard of in other times, there are many opportunities for spiritual advancement. Relative to much of the world, we live like kings and queens, princes and princesses. It is an extraordinary time where material prosperity is greater than it has ever been. This supportive material base can allow consciousness to develop and grow and mature far beyond what would happen if you were born in Somalia or a place of great strife and poverty.

Many people who come to me are fallen yogis. Learning how to pick oneself up after a fall is a necessary part of this yoga. Falling is inevitable in the process of purification that can take many lifetimes. Each fall reveals the next level of hidden structures or negative patterns to be overcome; we rise up again and again. This is the process of the spiritual journey. Again and again we fall, only to rise again. Dejection leads to discrimination, allowing us to correct our actions to recover what has been lost. It is an ongoing process of recognition of your remaining bondage. It is in this process that we gain the discrimination, strength, and maturity to traverse this path.

BE A YOGI!

279. *A yogi is superior to an ascetic, greater than a scholar, and also superior to a man of ritualistic worship. Therefore, Arjuna, be a yogi.*

280. *Of all the yogis, however, one who is ever linked with Me in heart and for Me has love and faith, him I consider to be the greatest and most dear to Me.*

Realizing the Self is no small feat. This is a significant milestone along the way. Coming to the Self is a true resting point in the evolution of consciousness, a platform where one can either put attention on the human life or turn attention to what is next. The tendency in Western culture, with its dominance on mind, senses, and sense pleasures full of distractions, is for one who is in this state to be distracted endlessly in the world, veiling their connection to their greater Self.

This completes the first part of the Bhagavad Gita, the first of the three phases, the movement of ego to the Self. The second six chapters is the movement of the Self to the universal as either God or Truth. The third six chapters is the integration of the awakened individual with universal states and the manifestation of this truth. These first six chapters are dependent upon our personal effort. This is where we consciously dismantle our self, the separate egoic existence, and build a relationship with the true Self that lives us.

If one is graced to have a teacher or a teaching that points to a higher state of consciousness, one can make it through this resting point and continue on the journey. To try to complete the entire journey in one lifetime should be the goal of any sincere aspiring seeker, because you never know what is going to happen in the next life. With that cautionary note we have completed the first six chapters of the Yoga of the Bhagavad Gita, and *The Bhagavad Gita Revealed: A Living Teaching for Our Times, Part 1.* The entire map of awakening is described in the Bhagavad Gita and is available online for free at my website, www.satshree.org.

I invite you to grow into this opportunity to manifest your highest potential so you can discover your part in this shift in collective consciousness that is under way. There can be no greater fulfillment than to give yourself over to such a work.

(The entire map of awakening as described in the Bhagavad Gita is available online for free at www.satshree.org.)

Appendices

Appendix I

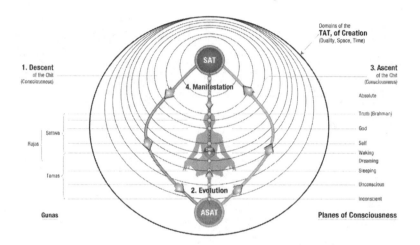

1. **Descent**
of the Chit
(Consciousness)

Sattwa

Rajas

Tamas

Gunas

Domains of the
TAT, of Creation
(Duality, Space, Time)

SAT

4. **Manifestation**

Chit

2. **Evolution**

ASAT

3. **Ascent**
of the Chit
(Consciousness)

Absolute

Truth (Brahman)

God

Self

Waking

Dreaming

Sleeping

Unconscious

Inconscient

Planes of Consciousness

THE JOURNEY OF CONSCIOUSNESS

Appendix II

THE MAIN CHARACTERS OF THE GITA

The Bhagavad Gita takes place on a battlefield. On one side are the mighty forces of the Pandava family, who represent the forces of light, and on the other side are the equally powerful forces of the Kaurava family, who represent the forces of darkness. The battle scene is an analogy of the inner battle of one who enters the spiritual path. As Arjuna is about to wage a war that will destroy the world as he has known it, so too must we, as the new seeker, overcome the resistance of the old way of life for the new one that awaits us.

The first twenty verses of the Gita describe a battle scene with an array of characters: kings, generals, and warriors poised for combat. This scene and these characters are representative of aspects of the ignorance that binds us. The battle scene described here is an analogy for the battle in consciousness. The battle is between the forces that cling to the old life—the world of mind and senses—and the forces that transcend these, the forces of light, love, and truth. The following is a list of the key characters and what they represent.

Krishna is Arjuna's charioteer. His role is only to guide the chariot, not to fight. He represents the Divine on earth, the spiritual teacher who guides us. He represents the grace, that mysterious unseen force, that brings to us the situations of life that are the opportunities to transform ourselves. Krishna represents the Supreme on earth, the Divine in human form.

Arjuna is a warrior and friend to Krishna. He represents the awakened (awakening?) seeker who actually fights the battle of transformation. It is the seeker that fights the battle. This is the battle of Gita, to overcome the inner and outer qualities that prevent our spiritual progress.

Sanjaya narrates the Gita and represents the inner conscience that can see the truth even when it does not want to be seen, the power of discerning introspection.

The Field of Kuru is the battlefield where the story of Gita takes place. It represents the field of action, where we work out this struggle of manifesting spirit in our lives.

The Kaurava Family represents the forces of ignorance and darkness that limit the consciousness to the old life. Loyalty, idealism, ethics, and morality are all seemingly noble qualities, but attachment to these binds the mature soul to the world of mind and senses, of friends, family, society, and culture. They operate from the lower vital and subconscious aspects of the mind, the lower sense mind. The qualities that are represented are as follows:

Dhritatashtra, the blind king, represents blind attachment and the surface mind, the superficial self only concerned with the world and its own desires, habits, and attachments.
Duryodhana represents the seat of desire-driven ego; the seat of the lower self; the most formidable opponent to the transformation process.

Drona represents misplaced loyalty; one who has compromised his higher Self for material security; one who acts out of habit and fear.

Kripa represents ethics and morality, right and wrong, sin and virtue. He stands for the rules of conduct that are based on dogma and fear.

Karna represents idealism based on mind and ego. Ideas are mental concepts that prevent us from knowing truth.

The Pandava Family symbolizes the forces of light. They are representative of a mature and positive human system capable of discerning between what is true and what is false; a system whose attributes include a developed psychic, an inspired vital, a discriminating intellect, a pure heart, and a healthy body. Arjuna is one of five Pandava brothers. They represent the qualities that support us on the spiritual path. They are introduced in verses fourteen through sixteen.

Arjuna represents the ideal man of his time; open and with discriminating intelligence and divine self-control.

Yudhishthira represents the developed psychic nature; the developed psychic man with divine calmness.

Bhima represents the inspired higher vital centered in the heart.

Sahadeva represents the intuitive nature and hidden intuition.

Nakula represents the pure and strong physical nature of man.

The entry into the spiritual path is not an easy one for most of us. It starts by throwing our lives into turmoil and anguish. The tendency is very strong to run away, but this would be an error. If we don't run away and if we stay the course, what arises is the aspiration to find out what is happening to us. This throws us into a quest for something—what that is, we do not fully know at this point. It is this quest that takes us to the next step in the journey.

Appendix III

THE GUNAS

Gunas are our moods, the coloring or veils that distort our ability to know and experience reality as it is. They shape the character of our personality and influence how we see the world. The gunas are within us and all about us. They are the field of environmental vibrations we swim in, and they reside in each of us in different components of our system. These forces that pervade all human dynamics are constantly interacting with each other.

Recognizing the characteristics of the gunas and the guna cycles is an important tool for separating ourselves from our egoic identity. Just as understanding the structure of the human system can allow us to see how the vehicle of our consciousness shapes our identity, so too does understanding that the gunas assist us in recognizing how we get caught up in the dynamic process of living life.

The first part of recognizing the gunas requires you to observe your own system and to identify which is the dominant guna. This is your base guna. The second part is to understand the three different guna cycles, and then observe and track which guna is active in your system at any given time. The gunas are experienced through the components of the human system.

One of the ways we can recognize which guna is our dominant guna is through the nature of our experiences.

IDENTIFYING OUR DOMINANT GUNA IN THE VITAL AND THE MENTAL

The dominant guna is the one that appears strongest in our system most of the time. Each of us has a dominant guna in the vital component and another in the mental component of our system. Thus, our nature might be rajas/tamas or tamas/rajas, depending on which guna is dominant in the vital and which guna is dominant in the mental components of our human system.

The three most important components of the human system relative to the gunas are the mental, the vital, and the physical. The mental rules thought, the vital rules feeling, and the physical rules sensation.

Use the following information to help you identify which guna is dominant in each component. Start with the vital and see which guna seems strongest in your system. Then look at the mental and see which one is strongest there. The physical is listed to help distinguish the guna's influence on the physical component from the more important vital and mental components.

The **vital** is the domain of feelings and action. It has the most power. Which guna do you identify most strongly with in your vital?

When one is in **sattwa** one feels inspiration, a pull to harmony, to nature spirits, and the spiritual path. One is optimistic, open, happy, feeling joy and connection with one's being.

Rajas drives one to action to fulfill ones desires, restlessness, and passion. One is material-minded, controlling, willful, frustrated or angry, and creative.

Tamas in the vital causes one to be negligent, sleepy, stubborn, lazy, and to procrastinate. One acts out of habit, looks for sense enjoyment, and tries to avoid fear and discomfort.

The **mental** is the domain of thoughts. See which guna you operate out of mostly in the mental.

Sattwa is the most subtle, the closest to the origin. One has mental clarity, enhanced understanding, insights, thoughts of God and Truth and an awareness of spaciousness, natural peace, and quiet.

In **rajas** one has thoughts about actions, problems, challenges, and how to expand in the material world and acquire more money, power, and control. Anxious thinking is often present.

In **tamas** one's consciousness is veiled in ignorance and one's thoughts are about bodily pleasure, resentments, complaints, gossip, judgments, and narrow thinking.

The **physical** is the domain of the body and senses. This domain is of a secondary influence.

In **sattwa** the body feels light, subtle, transparent, and there is a sense of physical well-being. There is an attraction to physical beauty, grace, perfection, artistry, and form.

When one is in **rajas** the body feels energized, active, restless, irritated, and hot or cold.

In **tamas** the body feels heavy, dull, and inclined toward unconsciousness and accidents. It is susceptible to illness, weakness, aches, and is pulled to sleep and sensuality.

There are four major guna cycles: daily, lunar, solar, and cosmic. By recognizing them, we can measure our process of transcendence. These cycles proceed naturally according to the balance of the gunas in our innate nature.

The **daily cycle** is much like the elements cycle. Every two hours—120 minutes—we tend to shift from one guna phase to another. Gunas shift in a sequence from sattwa to rajas to tamas to sattwa to rajas to tamas and so on. Start with the guna that is most noticeable in your system and track the sequence from that guna.

The **lunar cycle** is the cycle of gunas that changes between each phase of the moon. Approximately every fourteen days, from the new moon to full moon, or full moon to new moon, the gunas will perform a complete cycle. The way to discover your cycle is to note your experience. There will be a trend. If you find yourself entering a sattwa phase at a new moon, then track if it occurs again in that fourteen-day cycle. The number of days you spend in each guna will be equal at first, then sattwa will increase and rajas and tamas will decrease as you proceed on the path of transcendence.

The **solar cycle** is the cycle of gunas that changes due to the earth's annual rotation around the sun. Just as seasons shift from winter to spring, summer, and autumn, so does the influence of the gunas shift with each season. You can recognize this cycle by noticing how each of the seasons impacts you. For example, winter may be sattwa, a time of inwardness, turning to rajas in the spring and summer, becoming tamas in the fall. Each person will be influenced by these changing seasons according to where they are in their cosmic cycle.

The **cosmic cycle** is the cycle of gunas that occurs throughout one's lifetime. These cycles last for six, nine, or twelve years. It is possible to see them by looking back and contemplating the events of your life. From the nature of the events you can see if the event was during a sattwic, rajasic, or tamasic phase of that cycle. Peak periods where matters of spirit are expanding in importance are the sattwic phases; periods of expansion in the world of matter are the rajasic phases; periods of complete involvement in the physical world of senses are the tamasic phases. Each cosmic cycle will include a period in sattwa, then in rajas, then in tamas, then in sattwa again and so on.

Becoming aware of these cycles in our systems is an important step in transcending the gunas.

Appendix IV

The Components of the Human System

The Physical

The Physical sheath consists of the gross body, which is the outermost and most gross layer of the Human System. It is the abode of the five senses, which are the instruments for gathering impressions and experiences from the world of Matter. The Body is the physical vessel or "frame" that holds the rest of the Human System. It is the culmination of the evolutionary process, and it is the most sophisticated vehicle for experience in the entire Creation. It is a Microcosm of the entire Creation.

The Vital

The Vital is both the individual life force and the seat of direct experience. It records these experiences, storing them as impressions (vasanas) and inclinations (samsaras). The Vital is the seat of emotions, feelings, and action drives. These act like coiled springs which when activated release their energy suddenly, in a rush. It is the beginning of the Subtle body. The Vital strongly influences the physical body and is directly connected to the Mental component.

The Vital is the motivating force of one's life. All experience is felt powerfully in this component. It motivates one to act, to express oneself. It drives one to human relationship, infatuation and attachment, attraction and repulsion.

The Vital has two aspects, a lower Vital and a higher Vital. The lower Vital is the seat of desire, passion, and action. The higher Vital is the seat of higher human emotions, as well as aspiration, inspiration, and divine love.

The Mental

The Mental is the seat of the mind, memory, and the projector. It is the source of thoughts, our point of view of life, and our attitudes. It is the seat of the Subtle karmic body. The Mental records everything that it receives from the senses: impressions, thoughts, reactions, and responses. It gathers information from the senses, sorting, organizing, and storing everything. In a way it makes "sense" of the senses, "creating" the outer world.

The mind gathers all this subjective information accumulated throughout one's life: the beliefs, opinions, judgments, the notions of right and wrong, assessments learned from direct experience through the Vital, or from others.

The Mental has two aspects, a lower Mental and a higher Mental. The lower Mental is the seat of automatic thoughts. The higher Mental is the seat of reason, understanding, and learning.

The Intelligence

The Intelligence is the seat of the buddhi or the awareness. It gives the mind the ability to create and objectify. It discriminates and sets goals, priorities, and standards. It allows choice and the application of the will. The Intelligence is the aspect of the human system that chooses and makes decisions. It is capable of objective observation. It is capable of overriding the impulses, reactions, and desires of the lower components. It can observe and learn. It can integrate these lessons into its life. The Intelligence is the source of will, the ability to change oneself and intervene in what would otherwise be the natural course of affairs. The Intelligence takes on the coloring of the dominant Component in the Human System. It serves the desires or the aspirations of that component.

THE EGO

The Ego is the basis of our Identity. It is the "I am." The Ego has only this characteristic. It has no other qualities of its own. This is the subtlest component of the Human System. It is the principle of self-referencing in space and time. It is the beginning of separateness without which there would be no Creation. The Ego allows Consciousness, the Chit, to be separate from the rest of the Creation and thus creates the possibility for knowing and experiencing.

THE PSYCHIC

The Psychic is a way of knowing the supersensory, that which is beyond the mind or five senses. It allows us to know something without knowing how we know it. It is the interface between the individual and the world around them, including the subtle dimensions of existence. It is man's early warning system that lets us know if there is danger or opportunity around.

In early man the psychic was very developed. You could say it was mankind's substitute for instinct. In animals instinct is rigid, but in mankind the psychic was open and flexible. But this capacity was diminished, and in many it was lost as mankind became civilized. The Psychic was important in the early spiritual traditions of indigenous cultures. It was what allowed them to know directly the interconnection of all things. The Psychic is also the vehicle that lets us know and experience things beyond the mind, such as contact with subtle planes, as well things such as intuition, insight, inspiration, and aspiration.

The Soul

The soul is not really a Component of the Human System. It is rather that which allows the Human System. It enables us to exist. It is what absolute vacuum is to the world of matter. It is something outside of the Creation. Yet paradoxically it resides in each self-aware being. It is beyond space and time. It was never born nor can it die. It is neither universal nor individual, yet it is both universal and individual. It cannot be destroyed. The soul is the foundation of our individual existence. It is our I am-ness, our intelligence and will, our ability to choose, to experience, and to know. It is because of all this that it is possible for man to realize the SAT, to become the SAT.

Glossary of Terms

Absolute—The Sat, the Brahman; the Supreme unmanifest; the Self-Existing Existence.

action—The manifestation of the Chit, consciousness in existence. That which animates all that lives. The means to create change, to progress, to evolve. The field of engagement, of effort. The power that has been given to self-awareness to bring together the human with the divine. *See also* karma.

ananda—Love or bliss; the experience of coming more fully into existence. A state of delight; a dynamic expression of beingness that is produced automatically when the Sat is united with the Tat; when the purusha and the prakriti merge.

Arjuna—The third Pandava brother; the symbol of the best individual of his period; the awakened being within; the pure one.

asat—The dark version of the Sat; the inherent potentiality of consciousness lost in matter.

aspiration—A desire that arises from the inner self for something greater; a drive to know or experience God or Truth.

atman—The one soul from which come all souls.

Aum—The Aum sound is the primal mantra. It is the human vocal equivalent of the vibration of existence, the three gunas. A+U+M: the equilibrium state of sattwa, rajas, and tamas. *See also* Om.

austerity—Voluntary penance done for purifying the consciousness. Austerities are of three types: physical, mental and verbal. *See also* tapas.

avatar—A being such as Krishna or Rama that comes to the world periodically to help the collective consciousness move into a new era. The descent of the Supreme Being into the material plane. *See also* Incarnation.

awakened being—An individual who is aware of the purpose of their embodiment. *See also* being.

awakening—A shift in consciousness from a lower state to a higher one, such as awakening from dream or sleep. A shift in one's sense of reality. One experiences one's Self and life newly. The process of self-discovery of the purpose of embodiment.

awareness—A state of pure consciousness without a particular focus.

becoming—The Creation. The process by which the Supreme Being manifests itself in innumerable forms.

being—An individual expression of the Supreme Being. The radiance of the individual soul.

Bhagavan—A title given to one who is recognized to have attained a state of spiritual perfection; the Divine embodied. Often used in reference to the Krishna or the Supreme Being.

bhakti (path)—The experience of divine love that pulls one to God. An experience of the higher vital. One of the three spiritual paths: jñana (knowledge), bhakti (love), and karma (action).

black hole—A description of the soul as a doorway between existence and that which is prior to existence.

bliss—An inner state in which the light of the Being is reflected in the vital plane; the experience of the joy of the Self that has no external cause.

body—The vehicle or vehicles that allow consciousness to experience and know existence in all domains of existence: physical, subtle, and causal.

Brahma—The creator god; one of a triad of gods composed of Brahma, Vishnu, and Siva. Although the name is similar, Brahma should not be confused with Brahman.

Brahman—The Absolute; the impersonal all-pervading radiant field of consciousness that holds the potentiality of the Sat in existence.

buddhi—The intelligence, a faculty of knowing that is higher than the rational thinking mind.

caste—The four classes of ancient Vedic society are the sudra (service class), the vaishya (merchant class), the Kshatriya (warrior class), and the Brahmin (spiritual class).

chakras—The seven energy centers located at the midline of the human body starting at the base of the spine and going up to the crown of the head.

channel—When an individual is transformed into a container that can hold and express the universal forces. *See also* instrument, collaborator.

Chit—Consciousness, the radiant manifestation of the Sat into the Tat.

collaborator—A developed spiritual being who chooses to assist in the manifestation of a greater spiritual being. Can also be an instrument or channel.

compassion, misplaced—Sympathy due to attachment or identification with a person whose issues match one's own. This can be an obstacle on the path of yoga. Through misplaced compassion one often enables the other's ego, thus interfering with the operation of natural law, thereby bringing the karma of that person to one's self.

components of the human system—*See also* human system.

consciousness, planes of—Objective domains that range from gross to subtle that allow subjective experience and knowing by one who is in the matching state of consciousness. Planes are the objective domains. States are the subjective experience of those domains.

consciousness, states of—Stages of spiritual development that one attains on the spiritual path. Ascending states or frequencies of awareness and/or experience.

dejection—Where the soul, the consciousness that has been associated with a body, becomes aware of its bondage viscerally below the surface awareness.

delusion—A dynamic state of ignorance; a process by which the all-knowing being forgets its true nature after embodiment.

demon—Asura; a gross form of intense negative energy, often responsible for causing destruction in the material plane.

destiny—Accumulated unspent karmas of the past birth. In the case of yoga, individual will is mightier than destiny.

determinate intellect—A state in which the intellect is one-pointed, My-minded. *See also* equanimity; stitha prajna.

dharma—The action that we take that is aligned with our innate nature and with the original intent of existence; the evolutionary movement of consciousness in the becoming.

discrimination—A capacity that awakens on the spiritual path that can discern truth from untruth. The ability to connect to the purpose of life that guides one's actions so one doesn't get distracted.

dispassion—The lack of passion. A strong feeling of withdrawal from objects of pleasure.

dispassion, natural—A state of spontaneous withdrawal from sense objects, experienced when the mind turns inward to the Self.

duty, ordained—Actions that are compatible to the innate nature of a person and must be performed. Depending on the innate nature and the level of attainment in yoga, the ordained duty or karma may differ from person to person.

ego—The basis of our identity, the "I am." *See also* The Components of the Human System in the Appendix.

ego-ing—The activity of the ego. The endless wanting and grasping based on desire and fear and striving to preserve its own separate identity in the world of content.

egoism—A force of the individual willfulness coming through the vital that brings passion and anger to the activity of the ego, creating greater obscurity; that which is undivine and counter to the evolutionary purpose.

embodiment—The taking of a physical body.

enlightenment—The illumination of consciousness as it moves into relationship with Self, God, or Truth. A state in which the light of the Supreme pervades all the layers of consciousness; a state of complete freedom from prakriti. *See also* liberation.

equanimity—A state that leads to stitha prajna; a state of inner calmness that comes when one experiences the Self through samadhi in which one is indifferent to pain and pleasure, joy and sorrow, fame and defamation. *See also* Samadhi and stitha prajna.

evil—Any action that takes one away from God.

evolution—The process through which the purpose of life is fulfilled. Prakriti expands creation; the natural laws governing the cycle of creation. There are three stages of the evolutionary process: the formation of Matter, of Life, and of Mind. Each builds on the other.

fate—Destiny; the result of accumulated samskaras or tendencies for action karmas.

Gita—The song of the Supreme that lifts consciousness to Itself; a scripture on yoga in poetic dialogue format; a scripture that contains the essence of the Vedas and the gist of the Upanishads.

Gita, yoga of—A systematic and integral path that includes the yoga of action, the yoga of devotion, and the yoga of knowledge. It is composed of stages that lead to the supreme state.

God—The universal divine being that oversees all existence. Also known as the Supreme Being.

God-realization—Occurs when an individual being merges with the universal being, or God, taking on its attributes.

gods—Refers to deities, emanations, and celestial heavenly bodies.

grace—God's love; the force beyond the gunas that effects the transformation.

gunas—The threefold modes or attributes of prakriti: sattwa, rajas, tamas; the forces responsible for the cycles of creation.

guru—A spiritual guide or teacher. There are many levels of guru, depending on the stage of one's attainment.

guru force—A force beyond the gunas that accelerates the transformation process in those open to it. Not all gurus carry the guru force. *See also* Sat force.

heaven—A place of paradise in the subtle world. One goes to heaven through accumulation of good karma. It is not a permanent place for the soul, for one is bound to return to the world of karma when the merits are exhausted in heaven.

hell—A place of torture in the subtle world; a zone of darkness.

human system, components of—The total structure that holds the soul, the Being. It has seven different components: the physical, the vital, the mental, the intelligence, the ego, the psychic, and the soul. *See also* The Components of the Human System in the Appendix.

impressions—The subtle presence of karmas that come from the world of prakriti; stored up memories of past karmas. *See also* vasanas.

inaction—Inaction is not absence of action but the conscious withdrawal from the impulse for action. A dynamic state of action when the result of action is surrendered to Divine.

innate nature—The individual collection of inclinations and drives that one is born to release and work out. One's unique mix of the three gunas. *See also* ordained duty.

Incarnation—The Supreme Being or its emanation, manifesting through a form in response to the call of Mother Earth by descending to earth. *See also* avatar.

infatuation—The pull of the mind toward an object, due to allowing the mind to dwell on the objects of pleasure.

inquiry—A process of turning inward to find the root of what is arising in one's mind, vital, or body that has distorted or overtaken one's consciousness.

instrument—A spiritually developed individual who knowingly or unknowingly acts on the prompting of a higher purpose, being, or force. *See also* channel, collaborator.

Integral Yoga—Includes the yoga of action, knowledge, and devotion. *See also* Yoga, integral.

intellect—An aspect of the human mind that can think objectively and rationalize. Not the same as intelligence.

intelligence—The seat of the buddhi or awareness; beyond the mind; knowing without thinking. *See also* The Components of the Human System in the Appendix.

jiva—The eternal unchanging awareness associated with the individual evolving being, but which itself does not change. The individual spark of the Sat, the Absolute, that brings intelligence and self-awareness.

jivatman—The embodied being; the individual who is self-aware; the individual soul.

jñana—Knowledge; the direct awareness of the Supreme; experienced knowledge.

jñana yoga—A process of union with the being through the approach of knowledge.

kali yuga—There are four different eras of the creation that the Hindus call yugas: satya, treta, dwapara, and kali. Kali is furthest from the truth.

karma—Action, also the result or consequence of action. The sum total of a person's actions that determine the person's next incarnation. A force or law of nature that causes one to reap what one sows.

karma yoga—The yoga of action. A yogic technique of performing action as a sacrifice, without attachment to the fruits of one's actions or a sense of doership.

Krishna—The Supreme Being; that which attracts everything toward Him; the Blessed Lord Who revealed the teachings of the Yoga of Bhagavad Gita. *See also* avatar.

Krishna consciousness—A state of awareness; the consciousness of the Supreme Being; unity consciousness; the dynamic cosmic consciousness through a human form.

kundalini—Vital Shakti force lying dormant in the human body at the base of the spine.

kundalini yoga—The process of raising the kundalini energy upward from the base of the spine so that it crosses all the chakras.

Kurukshetra—The field of action; a field near modern Delhi where the battle of the Mahabharata was fought; the human system.

liberation—The state of freedom from the forces of prakriti; the process of release from the law of karma; freedom from the cycle of birth and death after merger with Supreme. *See also* enlightenment.

love—An expression of the being. An emotion based on the principle of self-giving, enriching the person. Love is divine but it is contaminated when it enters the world of senses and is expressed in relative terms, i.e., parental love, conjugal love, etc.

Mahabharata—Refers to the greatest epic of man, which is said to have consisted of 100,000 verses divided into eighteen parts in which the Bhagavad Gita, the celestial song, comes in the ninth part, the very middle of the epic.

manifestation—Expression of the divine through the body, mind, and intellect.

mantra—A psychic vibration; a rhythm of cosmic sound waves which activates the psychic and neutralizes thought waves of other planes.

masters, enlightened—Persons who have descended back to the world of matter after experiencing nirvikalpa samadhi.

maya—The apparency of things including illusion and delusion. It is that which makes the real appear unreal and the unreal appear real.

meditation—A technique of yoga where one turns one's attention inward, away from outward things onto the inner being or self.

merger—The state of union of consciousness with Itself. There are three stages: merger with the Self, merger with God or the Supreme Being, and merger with the Absolute.

middle kingdom—The unmanifest subtle planes of consciousness above the gross physical, from the subtle physical to the vital and mental planes where demigods, great beings, and gods reside. These can be directly experienced by one who is on the path to God realization. These are referenced in Chapter 11 of the Bhagavad Gita. *See also* consciousness, planes of and states of.

nirvana—A state of awareness when the individual consciousness merges with the universal unmanifest. A complete withering away of the individual into the state of the Absolute. The goal of the Buddhist path.

nirvikalpa samadhi—The final samadhi. A state in which the individual awareness is permanently merged with the Supreme Being in all planes of consciousness and in all parts of his or her system. *See also* samadhi.

nivritti—The tendency of consciousness to turn inward and grow inwardly; the inclination that takes one away from the objects of pleasure.

no-self—The absence of the activity of the usual ego, thinking, feeling, etc. Abiding in the state of no separation, the nondual state.

Om—The original vibration that comes from that which has no origin, no ending, no meaning—the Sat. The sound produced in the cycle of creation, from which the Creation arises. Creation is always manifesting the Om. *See also* Aum.

Om Tat Sat—This is the subject matter of Gita. Om is the manifestation of the original vibration that arises from the union of the Sat with the Tat. Tat is the manifest and unmanifest creation, also God. Sat is the Absolute, that unspeakable potentiality prior to existence. The yoga of Gita takes us to that perfect perfection, that three-dimensional, threefold realization of Om Tat Sat.

Original Intent—The will to be, to exist, that arose from the Sat. The potentiality for existence to manifest the innumerable possibilities for being in matter. *See also* purpose.

ordained duty—The path of yoga that is predetermined for each person based upon his or her innate nature. One should follow that path and not jump to another that is not ordained because it could prove disastrous. *See also* innate nature.

prakriti—The Tat, the Creation, space, time, and casualty. The content of existence, both manifest and unmanifest, including the gods, humans, and all that is. On an individual level it is our personality, our ego, our mind's ideas, thoughts, beliefs, our vital moods, feelings, and desires. It is our body sensations and experiences.

prana—Vital air, the life force.

pranayama—The technique of breath control.

pravritti—The tendency of consciousness to turn outward, to grow and evolve into existence. The inclination that takes one towards the objects of pleasure.

pressure—Feeling of resistance or heaviness, mostly felt on the head or chest during or after meditation. The descent of Sat below the psychic plane forcibly tries to reject all that resists it.

process—An action that happens in time, which is automatic and natural, which requires no effort and which no effort can stop nor intensify. It is governed by the laws of creation both material and spiritual. Materially it is breathing, digestion, and circulation of the blood. Spiritually it is the natural unfolding of stages of the spiritual journey.

psychic—The interface between the soul and the personality. The part of the human system that knows without thinking. A field of being that allows us to know and experience things beyond mind and senses. *See also* The Components of the Human System in the Appendix.

purpose—The current of existence that arises from the Original Intent to exist, to BE, to learn, grow, evolve, and eventually wake up to its own nature.

purusha—The being. The knower and the experiencer of creation, the individuality both at the individual and universal level. *See also* prakriti.

Purushottama—The Supreme Being, the ultimate Purusha.

rajas—One of the modes of prakriti that activates the action drive, producing desire, restlessness, and passion, and the desire to acquire more money, power, and control. *See also* The Gunas in the Appendix.

realization—The integration of one's attainment in all the parts of one's system that allows that which previously was coming and going to become real; one is able to know directly one's true nature as the Self, God, and/or the Supreme.

rebirth—A part of the process of the soul's journey from life to life when it takes a physical body.

recognition—The ability to sense Truth or God without knowing why. The pull to Truth or God.

reincarnation—The idea of the continuity of the consciousness through lifetime after lifetime.

renunciation—To organize oneself in a more consecrated way so that one can be sustained in one's willingness to apply the effort required to renounce the urges that rise up within our human nature from the pull of the senses and the impulses of the lower vital.

revelation—A state of consciousness that instantly knows the nature of that which it is focusing on or attending to. A state of seeing or knowing that allows the truth of something to reveal itself.

sacrifice—The effort to change from what you are inclined to do to something that is aligned with your intelligent will. An offering to something higher or truer.

sadhana—Spiritual practice.

saint—One who knows the Self or God and surrenders their life to living continuously in that state, becoming pure and selfless in the process.

samadhi—The Sanskrit word for this is stitha prajna, which means stable intelligence. It is when the consciousness has turned its attention away from the outer world and has become absorbed in its own nature in a stable way.

Samkhya yoga—A yogic method to reach the state of the being by focusing on the soul, the purusha, and bypassing prakriti, the world.

samsara—The ever-changing ocean of collective impressions and drives to action (vasanas and samskaras) that bind consciousness to the domains of the creation, subtle to gross.

sannyasa—Renunciation; a withdrawal from desire-prompted activities, leading the way to freedom from the law of karma. *See also* tyaga.

sannyasi—One who attains an inner state of withdrawal from desire-prompted activities. Through this yogic state one is able to remain calm in the face of desire.

samskara—Behavioral tendency or karmic imprint which influences the present behavior of a person. The carried-over consequences of previous actions (residual karma) that creates a drive for continuing the action, often from past lives. Like a coiled spring, a suppressed samskara becomes powerful and after death will bring the consciousness back to the body, mind, intellect, or the vital for release. *See also* vasanas.

Sat—The Absolute beyond all qualities. The condition of non-existence that holds the potentiality for existence.

Sat force—A powerful and effective force of consciousness that originates beyond existence that awakens consciousness from its embedment with matter; converting untruth into truth. *See also* guru force.

satchitananda—Existence (Sat), consciousness (Chit), and bliss (Ananda); the current of existence that manifests the inherent will to be, exist, evolve, and wake up. When connected to this current one becomes a manifesting channel for it, bringing great presence, knowingness, and delight. The purusha and prakriti join integrally together, manifesting simultaneously through a form. *See also* The Components of the Human System in the Appendix.

sattwa—One of the three modes of prakriti; dwells in the psychic plane and takes the being toward its Source. *See also* The Gunas in the Appendix.

seeker—One who seeks God or Truth. When one wakes up to their bondage or to the awareness not bound to mind or senses, an aspiration comes to know and experience these. Also one who, due to the cycle of the gunas, is aware that there is something more to life and has embarked on the process of self-inquiry.

self—The bound being, the individual person, the human ego, the small self.

Self—The one unbound being which all selves are an expression of; our authentic Self: that quality of being aligned with the spiritual path which has an inherent intelligence and will with less human conditioning and attachment. *See also* being and purusha.

Self-realization—When one realizes the Self; the event that happens when one recognizes they have merged with Self. Also the merger of the individual self with the universal Self.

seva—Service; the process of self-giving through physical action that serves the enlightened being or guru; it is a powerful tool for self-purification and transformation.

Shakti—Force; dynamic expression of the current of existence that comes from the higher planes of consciousness. In Sanskrit Shakti is a feminine term; thus, it is the concept of the manifesting principle of the Divine Mother, or Nature.

siddha—One who has attained at least the state of the being; a master of yoga.

siddhi—A spiritual power gained through spiritual practices. Also one who has attained the state of the Self.

Shiva—One of the three main gods of Hinduism: Brahma (the creator), Vishnu (the preserver), and Shiva (the destroyer). Shiva stands aloof as the purusha, ever the witness, never allowing itself to step down into the dance of prakriti, the jñanatman. Shiva is the eternal Guru.

Soul—The source of the Supreme Being and of all individual souls. The individual soul is a piece of this, the source of individual self-awareness, and a vacuum or doorway through which the Sat manifests. The soul came into matter to manifest the original purpose of the Supreme, making the soul an intermediary, a channel. The soul is eternal, indestructible, imperishable, birthless, deathless, immortal, all-pervading Sat.

stitha prajna—Samadhi; a state when the buddhi or intellect is stabilized on the Self, on the being, on the Brahman. There are various levels of this state, depending on one's state of attainment. The first is the samadhi of the individual being. The last level is the samadhi of the Supreme Being, when all the levels of consciousness have become integrated. *See also* samadhi and equanimity.

Supreme Being—The Purushottama; the Lord of the whole creation through whom the current of satchitananda is manifest. It has no role to play but to hold the space in the purposefulness of the Original Intent of existence. It can take an individual form as an Incarnation or avatar or express itself through multiple forms that are capable.

surrender—A spontaneous act of total self-giving; a reaching up to something greater than yourself for it to reveal itself or to reveal what is hidden or blocked.

tamas—One of the threefold modes of prakriti which clouds the being and diminishes the ability of consciousness to manifest its purpose. Activates the lower or more primitive qualities that come from nature. If left unchecked it causes dissolution, inaction, obscurity, ignorance, and unconsciousness. *See also* The Gunas in the Appendix.

tapas—The quality of strength to persevere, to show restraint, and endure calmly. It is the practice of saying "no" to your human habit or to your animal inclinations.

Tat—That or this-ness. The domain of all that is or happens. It defines the domain of the manifestation of the Sat.

transcendence—A yogic technique by which a person goes beyond the gunas, overcoming the pull of tamas, the push of rajas, and the bliss of sattwa. The ability to go beyond the pull of the mind and senses so that one is able to stay connected to the inner Self or a higher state of consciousness.

transformation—The means by which the individual ancestral karmas and innate limitations are undone, allowing for greater integration of spirit in matter. In this process Sat descends through the layers of the system and rejects and dissolves all that resists its descent, causing turbulence that can impact all parts of the system. It's the automatic process that occurs when the Sat force descends into one's system—transmuting untruth into truth, selfishness into selflessness, fear into faith—so that the true purpose of existence can manifest more perfectly.

Truth—That which is beyond time and space, the unchanging Now, the Absolute, the Sat. Also the all-pervading impersonal field of consciousness; Brahman.

tyaga—The act of offering the results of action to the Supreme; in tyaga, unlike renunciation, action is not given up, thus expressing past tendencies for action without creating new ones. *See also* sannyasa.

tyagi—One who practices tyaga. A true tyagi does not withdraw himself or herself from action but only performs those actions that are necessary or required without a result motive or seeking any particular result. The tyagi differs from the sannysasi, who does withdraw from outer action.

vasanas—Impressions or experiences collected through the course of lifetimes. These may accumulate during some lives, gathering a direction or motive for action. Samskaras are the tendencies and vasanas are the impressions. *Also see* samskaras.

vibhuti—An emanation from the universal. An expression of the one divine nature that pervades everything.

vital—The seat of emotions, feelings, and action drives. It has two aspects, the lower and the higher. *See also* The Components of the Human System in the Appendix.

yoga—The conscious and willful action we take toward a purpose: to merge with the goal, to complete what we are striving for, to realize the Self or the Soul.

Yoga, Integral—A yoga path that includes the yogas of knowledge, of action, and of devotion. This method of yoga is described in the Bhagavad Gita and was perfected by the Mother and Sri Aurobindo, who emphasized perfection in human nature. The aim of Integral Yoga is not realization of Divine only in the psychic plane, but in the entire human system.

yogamaya—One of the distorting expressions of maya that makes the real seem unreal and the unreal seem real. The illusions, distortions, or veils that the individual or collective ego puts on a striving yogi, preventing them from progressing on the spiritual path.

yogi—One who is pursuing the path of yoga. Whether one is in the process stage or is still in the aspiring stage or has already merged, all three are on the yoga path and are called yogis.

yuga—A cycle of time in the creation having four periods from high to low: Satya, Treta, Dwapara, and Kali. Each period defines the possibilities for that era to manifest the purpose of the creation. Each yuga has a different capacity for those alive during those times, to manifest spirit in matter. The Supreme Being as the avatar often descends into matter in each of these periods as needed in order to assure the purpose and steady progression of the evolutionary intent.

88276356R00156

Made in the USA
San Bernardino, CA
11 September 2018